People and Performance in Knowledge-Intensive Firms

A comparison of six research and technology organisations

Juani Swart

Nicholas Kinnie

John Purcell

Work and Employment Research Centre (WERC), School of Management, University of Bath

First published 2003

Cover design by Curve
Designed and typeset by Paperweight
Printed in Great Britain by Short Run Press

British Library Cataloguing in Publication Data:
A catalogue record for this book is available from the British Library

ISBN 0 85292 976 5

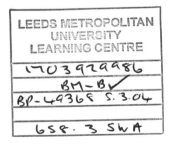

Chartered Institute of Personnel and Development
CIPD House, Camp Road, London, SW19 4UX

Tel.: 020 8971 9000
Fax: 020 8263 3333
E-mail: www.cipd.co.uk

incorporated by Royal Charter: Registered charity no. 1079797.

Contents

Acknowledgements

We would like to extend our sincere gratitude to the CIPD for funding this research. In particular we want to thank Angela Baron for her continued support and patience during the research process.

This research would not have been possible without the participation and knowledge-sharing with our case organisations. In each organisation all the managers and employees were extremely helpful, yet we acknowledge that the research co-ordinators in each acted as ambassadors for the research, and their enthusiasm encouraged participation. In particular we would like to thank:
John Wild and Suzanne Hall-Gibbons at Epinet
Mark Rowse, David Callcott and Susan Corry at Ingenta
Jane Roberts and Roger Smith at Marlborough Stirling
David Sherrif, Claire Groom and Eleri Joyce at Microgen-Kaisha
Steve Harper, Phil Buckley and Simon Pooley at MPC Data
Laurence Ede, Hugh Cookson and Dave Sunter at Tocris Cookson

Finally we would like to thank Cathy Aubin at the School of Management for her patience in combining various electronic documents and for spending several hours on data input. These building blocks made the research possible.

Foreword

This report is the first in a series of publications detailing the results from a three-year study commissioned by the Chartered Institute of Personnel and Development from the University of Bath. The research team has collected a wealth of data on a number of issues, including detailed employee attitudinal data and a range of performance data within each of the participating organisations. This particular report focuses on the results from a group of organisations in the emerging knowledge-intensive sector.

The Bath study forms the final and most important piece of work in the Institute's on-going investigation into the relationship between people management and business performance. Since launching this work in 1997 the CIPD has focused on three specific aims:

◘ to improve the evidence linking people management to business performance or organisational competitiveness

◘ to improve understanding of why and how people management practices influence business performance

◘ to provide accessible information on which managers can act through effective choices and decisions.

We have published a series of research reports, books and articles to date, including:

◘ *The Impact of People Management Practices on Business Performance – A literature review* (1999) by Ray Richardson and Marc Thompson

◘ *Effective People Management* (2000) by David Guest, Jonathan Michie, Maura Sheehan, Neil Conway and Melvina Metochi

◘ *Performance through People: The new people management* (2001), a CIPD change agenda paper

◘ *Voices from the Boardroom* (2001) by David Guest, Zella King, Neil Conway, Jonathan Michie and Maura Sheehan-Quinn.

This piece of work falls firmly into the middle category, having as its initial research aim an investigation of the 'black box' between HR and performance. With this work we will be able to strengthen the arguments about causality and improve understanding of how the relationship works in specific circumstances and environments.

The knowledge-intensive sector was chosen for special investigation because it reflects likely changes in the UK economy in the future. Knowledge-intensive work has become increasingly important over the last decade or so, and is challenging widely held beliefs about how organisations should be structured and managed.

The original intention of the work was to discover whether knowledge-intensive firms which are relatively young, small and fast-growing are developing a model for people management which is different from that of larger, more established organisations. The organisations chosen for study are populated largely by knowledge workers, and the knowledge of those workers is inextricably linked with the product or service they offer – which is, for example, software design, consultancy or creative solutions. This study has been conducted alongside and following the same methodology as a larger study drawing on information from 12 major companies in a range of sectors. The results are therefore discussed in the light of the larger study.

The results clearly show that a new model of people management is emerging in knowledge-intensive firms. This model plays a key role in developing the kind of intellectual and social capital these firms need in order to acquire business and manage customer relationships. The authors conclude that it is not just the knowledge and skills of the workforce that is critical but also the knowledge-sharing processes within the firm which help maximise the benefit of their expertise for the firm.

In 2003 we shall be publishing the results from the main study, including the Ability, Motivation and Opportunity (AMO) model which explains the relationship between people management practices and performance outcomes.

The CIPD has been working in the area for five years, and the academic research is now drawing to a close. We are confident that we have demonstrated compelling reasons why good people management really does make a difference to the bottom line. The challenge now is to turn that evidence into everyday reality reflected in all business decision-making.

Angela Baron

Adviser Organisation and Resourcing
Chartered Institute of Personnel and Development

Executive summary

Knowledge-intensive firms are increasingly important in developed economies and have a number of distinctive organisational and market characteristics which challenge traditional ways of managing and organising.

This report studies those organisations which employ a high proportion of knowledge workers, are engaged in work which applies expertise to novel problems, and provide services for business clients, sometimes in collaboration with partners in an external network.

People management practices are especially important in these organisations because they rely completely on various forms of knowledge held by their employees to compete successfully.

There are three 'knowledge situations' that are critical to the success of these firms:

◘ developing individual knowledge and skills

◘ sharing and developing this knowledge within the organisation

◘ sharing and developing this knowledge with clients and other parties in the network.

People management processes play a key role in managing these knowledge-intensive situations successfully – in particular, those concerned with:

◘ recruiting, developing, rewarding and retaining key employees

◘ developing forms of social capital to facilitate the sharing of knowledge within the organisation

◘ developing processes for acquiring client and market capital and for managing relationships with clients and other partners.

The success of our organisations as measured by a variety of indicators is a reflection of their ability to manage the tensions that are created between the needs of knowledge workers and the requirement to share knowledge between competing team, organisational, professional and client identities, and between the need for formal HR policies and more informal approaches to the management of employees.

Successful knowledge-intensive firms (KIFs) overcome these tensions by ensuring that the way they manage their people supports and enhances their practices and processes for developing and sharing knowledge. These firms gain an intellectual capital advantage by achieving a mutually supportive HR advantage.

1 | Introduction

There is now widespread evidence of an association between the adoption of high-commitment people management practices and improvements in organisational performance.[1] However, considerable uncertainty remains over how and why people management[2] practices have this effect. The Work and Employment Research Centre at Bath has been conducting research over the last three years, supported by the CIPD, to understand these links more clearly.

This research has involved two studies.

- ◘ The first looks at these issues of people and performance in 12 – mostly large – case studies, and will be published in 2003.

- ◘ The second, which grew out of the first, was motivated by a desire to look at these issues in small dynamic, knowledge-intensive firms (KIFs) which we know are becoming more important within developed economies (Frenkel *et al*, 1999).

Typical examples of KIFs include management, engineering and computer consultancy companies, advertising agencies, research-and-development units and high-tech companies.

Such organisations have a number of distinctive characteristics that are critical to the performance of the business. They operate in a pressure-cooker-type environment where product and labour markets are unstable and technology is changing quickly. They develop complex and innovative internal and external structures and forms which may provide a model for other more traditional large, slow-growing and relatively bureaucratic organisations.

Moreover, these firms treat knowledge and expertise as their trading assets which they seek to sell to clients. These knowledge-intensive organisations gain their competitive advantage by converting their human capital into intellectual capital in ways which create value in the marketplace and are difficult to imitate. Successful firms are able to offer services which draw on expertise that is scarce and difficult to substitute. In particular, they possess not only hard-to-find explicit knowledge (or 'know-what') but also tacit knowledge ('know-how') which is difficult to copy and distinctive to their organisation (Polanyi, 1967; Nonaka and Takeuchi, 1995).

Such organisational and environmental characteristics challenge traditional ways of organising based on hierarchy and specialisation and pose a whole series of questions about the people management practices that are most appropriate in these contexts. Ghoshal and Bartlett (1995: 96) suggest that this may require a shift from what they term the 'strategy-structure-systems' paradigm where the managerial task is largely concerned with allocating resources, assigning responsibilities and then controlling the outcomes to one based more on 'purpose-process-people' where the task is to

shape the behaviors of people and create an environment that enables them to take initiative, to co-operate and to learn.

Despite the importance of these firms and their distinctive characteristics, there are few empirical studies of such organisations, especially those which seek to link people management practices and performance. Ironically, these are the very kinds of organisation in which people management practices are more likely to have a direct effect on business performance than those used in manufacturing where plant and equipment differences are likely to be important and where

'There are three knowledge-intensive situations that are critical to the success of an organisation.'

there is less direct contact between employees and their customers.

Our study has become focused on a number of questions that we feel are central to the issues:

☐ What are the key characteristics of knowledge-intensive organisations?

☐ What are the particular knowledge-intensive situations that are important for the success of the organisation?

☐ Which people management practices are particularly valuable in helping to manage these situations successfully?

To answer these questions we have been conducting research in six knowledge-intensive companies over the last two years. The cases are described in Chapter 3, using a number of themes drawn from the existing research presented in Chapter 2. Following the outline of the cases we focus on the knowledge-intensive situations that are key to organisational success. Chapter 5 then examines the people management practices and processes that have been successfully employed to manage such situations in our cases. Finally, in Chapter 6 we consider the implications for the links between people management and performance in these organisations, and draw some wider conclusions.

Our main findings can be summarised as:

☐ There are three knowledge-intensive situations that are critical to the success of an organisation. These are:

    ☐ developing individual knowledge and skill

    ☐ sharing this knowledge within the organisation

    ☐ sharing this knowledge with other parties including clients, partners and suppliers.

☐ There are a series of people management practices and processes which play a key role in managing these knowledge-intensive situations[3] successfully. These are:

    ☐ attracting, developing, rewarding and retaining human capital

    ☐ recognising the importance of social capital

    ☐ building network management skills.

☐ When we examine the factors that contribute to organisational success in more detail, there is a series of tensions that are critical to business performance. These are the tensions between

    ☐ balancing the interests of individual knowledge workers and the need to share knowledge within and between organisations

    ☐ the need to identify with the employing organisation, the client and the client's profession

    ☐ the need for formal explicit policies and procedures and for more informal embedded practices.

☐ The best-performing organisations are those which are able to manage these three tensions successfully by ensuring that the way they

> '...current literature and practice indicate that the knowledge-based movement has a sense of permanence...'

manage their people supports the way they manage their knowledge.

- ☐ The successful companies achieve an HR advantage that contributes towards their intellectual capital advantage.

Before we look in more detail at the distinctive characteristics of these organisations, we would like to place this study in the context of the wider research in the field. The next section briefly reviews the theoretical roots of the research. Here we emphasise the importance of the knowledge-based view (KBV) of a firm in an understanding of the intricacies of knowledge-intensive firms.

The knowledge-based view of a firm

The notion of knowledge management, knowledge workers and knowledge-intensive firms has taken centre stage in management debate – approximately 320 relevant articles were published between 1994 and 1999 alone, and several journals dedicated to the topic (Scarbrough *et al*, 1999). The burgeoning field of knowledge is now also considered to have moved beyond fad status (Scarbrough and Swan, 2001).

In other words, current literature and practice indicate that the knowledge-based movement has a sense of permanence, and that we need to understand it better in order to develop the appropriate skill repertoire to manage knowledge effectively.

Drucker's (1993) seminal work suggests that knowledge is at the heart of the new economy, and claims further that in this knowledge-based economy, knowledge is not just another resource alongside the traditional factors but the *only* meaningful resource.

The issue of key resources that enable organisations to compete in their environment is central to the resource-based view (RBV) of a firm. It is not surprising, then, that resource-based theorists who recognise the importance of knowledge and experience argue that knowledge meets all the qualities of a desirable resource – it is valuable and scarce, inimitable, non-substitutable and appropriable (Boxall and Purcell, 2003). Knowledge-based resources are difficult to imitate and substitute because they are subtle and hard to understand (Grant, 1991). Both individual and organisational knowledge are therefore regarded as key influencers and/or determinants of firm performance.

The resource-based view of the firm values tacit knowledge (Polanyi, 1967) in particular: the know-how of employees is regarded as a critical firm resource. This notion of know-how has both a technical/professional and an organisation-specific dimension. It is the organisation-specific dimension that gives technical knowledge a unique quality and ensures that competitors cannot imitate the specific knowledge held in the organisation.

The pivotal role played by organisational tacit knowledge then extends the resource-based view of the firm to the knowledge-based view (KBV) by which organisational processes, embedded routines and systems are regarded as core competencies (Hamel and Prahalad, 1994). It is also believed that the KBV has greater utility in uncertain environments (Miller and Shamsie, 1996) such as are found in KIFs.

The knowledge-based view of the firm regards knowledge as the key asset in creating a competitive advantage. Knowledge is situated in organisational routines and processes, and is

'The growth of knowledge-intensive firms has been one of the most remarkable developments within modern economies...'

therefore distributed throughout the organisation (Tsoukas, 1996).

According to the knowledge-based view of the firm we can expect that economies of the future will be education-led or, as popularly referred to, will be knowledge-intensive. The growth of knowledge-intensive firms (KIFs) has also been one of the most remarkable developments within modern economies in recent years. Such organisations are likely to continue to proliferate and account for an increasing proportion of the highly skilled employment opportunities.

For example, top MBA recruits no longer find as many positions in manufacturing companies, but a high number secure positions with management consultants, accounting firms, software developers and information brokers (Bontis, 1998). These organisations operate in environments which are characterised by dynamic product and labour markets and fast-changing technologies.

Lei, Slocum and Pitts (1999: 26) argue that in tomorrow's business world, knowledge businesses such as design and engineering services, computer software design, high fashion, financial services, health care and management consulting will not only rely on the process of innovation but will require a continuous cycle that creates more dynamic markets for goods and services. According to these authors, knowledge-based firms will not only quickly respond to customers' needs but also actively shape their expectations for future products and services.

Having outlined the key questions addressed and the context of the study, we now consider the distinctive characteristics of KIFs and explain our methods of collecting data.

Endnotes

1   See for example Appelbaum *et al* (2000), Boxall and Purcell (2003), Pfeffer (1998).

2   We use the phrases 'people management' and 'human resources' (HR) interchangeably in this report.

3   See Chapter 4 for a definition and description of various knowledge-intensive situations.

2 | Knowledge-intensive firms – what makes them different?

This chapter identifies the distinctive characteristics KIFs possess, and contrasts them with the characteristics of larger, more traditional organisations that we have studied in the wider People and Performance research project. It also explains how our definition of KIFs shaped the way in which we designed and carried out our study.

The phrase 'knowledge-intensive' is problematic in that it can be defined in terms of:

◘ the type of the workforce employed

◘ the nature of work the employees are engaged in

◘ the characteristics of the industry or sector.

Furthermore, the distinction between knowledge-intensive and non-knowledge-intensive organisations or work is not self-evident (Alvesson, 2001).

Quinn (1992) has argued that all types of work and work organisations appear to involve knowledge: employees need a fair amount of know-what and know-how in order for any firm to create sustainable competitive advantage. This is complicated further by the difficulty in evaluating knowledge-intensive outcomes. How do we know whether a particular service or product is knowledge-intensive? Often these questions are answered not by the organisation or the knowledge workers themselves but by clients who 'buy' the particular products and services (Alvesson, 2001). However, in many crucial respects there are key differences between knowledge-intensive firms and more traditional and routinised organisations.

The category of knowledge-intensive firms (Alvesson, 1995, Robertson and Swan, 1998,

Starbuck, 1992) comprises firms where most of the work is said to be of an intellectual nature and where well-educated, qualified employees form the major part of the workforce. Furthermore, such companies reckon to produce 'qualified' products and/or services (Alvesson, 2000; 2001). Typical examples of KIFs include law and accounting firms, management, engineering and computer consultancy companies, advertising agencies, R&D units and high-tech companies (Alvesson, 2000).

These examples indicate that there is considerable overlap between KIFs and professional organisations, eg those of lawyers, accountants or physicians. Yet the category of KIFs is generally much broader than that of professional bodies and includes organisations with a more organisationally specific knowledge base (Alvesson, 2001; Robertson *et al*, 1999).

The distinctive characteristics of knowledge-intensive firms are revealed by considering

◘ the type of input or capital

◘ the nature of the work

◘ the market relations in the industry.

Knowledge intensity and the type of input/capital

The key resource in KIFs is often referred to as intellectual capital or the intellectual material – knowledge, information, intellectual property, experience – that can be put to use to create wealth (Stewart, 1997). Starbuck (1992) suggests that 'knowledge-intensive' can be applied to firms in which knowledge has more importance than other inputs, and in which human capital – as opposed to physical or financial capital – dominates.

> **'On average, more than 10 per cent of GDP in OECD countries is estimated to go into intangibles or intellectual capital.'**

Robertson and Hammersley (2000) argue further that knowledge is the primary asset of a knowledge-intensive firm. The movement towards value creation via intangible assets is supported by recent trends in investment patterns. During the 1990s the dominant investments were in R&D, education and competencies, IT software and the Internet (Lev, 1997). On average, more than 10 per cent of GDP in OECD countries is estimated to go into intangibles or intellectual capital (Edvinsson, 2000: 12).

The value that is created via intangible assets (knowledge) is also reflected in stock prices. In the late 1970s the average ratio between market value and book value was one to one, in the mid-1990s it had increased to an average of three to one, and now it is more than six times the book value. For some companies (eg AOL, Microsoft) around 90

per cent of their market capitalisation value is in intangibles (Lev, 1997).

In our research the flow of capital from human capital through to intellectual capital is seen to be an important factor in defining knowledge-intensive processes. Here we refer to intellectual capital models (Bontis, 1998; Snell, 2002) that demonstrate the centrality of human capital and by definition people management practices in the success and growth of KIFs. According to these models, intellectual capital comprises: human capital, structural/social capital, organisational capital, and customer capital (see Table 1).

Drawing on these various forms of capital, we set specific parameters in selecting our case organisations. Here we define 'knowledge intensity' as the extent to which an organisation

Table 1 | Forms of intellectual capital

Form of capital	Description
Human capital	Human intellect. Individual tacit knowledge, ie inarticulable skills necessary to perform individuals' functions (Nelson and Winter, 1982). Innovation, creativity and problem solution. Combination of genetics, education, experience and attitudes toward life and business.
Social capital	Knowledge embedded within the organisational relationships and routines (organisational tacit knowledge).
Structural capital	Structures that support the social relationships, ie networks or project teams.
Organisational capital	Technologies and processes, eg customer segmentation, software, customisation.
Client and market capital	Knowledge about the market and clients, and the processing for sharing this knowledge.

relies upon intangible assets to compete in the marketplace. A high reliance on intellectual capital was therefore used as an indicator of knowledge intensity.

This introduces an important dimension of knowledge intensity – for an organisation to rely on intellectual capital (rather than other forms of capital), the quality of human, social, organisational and customer capital must be high. The focus therefore shifts to the profile of the workforce.

A key differentiator of KIFs is the reliance on intangible assets or intellectual capital to create market wealth. Here intellectual capital includes human capital, social capital, organisational capital and structural capital. If intellectual capital is to play a central role in the organisation, it must be of exceptional quality.

Alvesson (2001) highlights the importance of the nature of the workforce and defines a KIF as a company where well-qualified employees form the major part of the workforce. The quality of human capital is important because it is a source of innovation and strategic renewal (Bontis, 1998).

We intended to focus on organisations in which the *nature of the work* is as knowledge-intensive as the *nature of the workforce*. In our study this excluded the professions because we regard professional services as subject to governance issues that may not necessarily involve knowledge intensity.

The nature of the work – applying intellectual capital

For KIFs to be a useful (and unique) category, one requirement is that exceptional expertise makes

important contributions (Starbuck, 1992).

A key characteristic of KIFs is said to be the capacity to solve complex problems through creative and innovative solutions. It is therefore not the mere presence of intellectual capital but also how it is applied that is important. The application of human capital highlights two important issues:

◘ Creative jobs, such as those of advertising executives, are not necessarily knowledge-intensive if they do not involve intricate problem solution.

◘ Standardised work is not regarded as knowledge-intensive, even if it requires high levels of intellectual capital. For example, the making of flutes (Yanow, 1999) of course requires a knowledge of flute-making, but its repetitive nature – by which the skills involved are eventually embodied – does not qualify as knowledge-intensive. In other words, doing a clever thing over and over does not mean that it is knowledge-intensive.

These parameters focused our selection on organisations where the routinisation of products/ services is limited. In other words, to focus on the influence of people management on performance in KIFs we relied heavily on the central role of people (tacit knowledge) rather than of procedures (explicit knowledge) in these organisations.

It can be argued that the output of the 'exceptional contribution that intellectual capital makes' is questionable. Firstly, the output is often intangible (for example, consulting advice) and its quality is difficult to determine. Whether a solution is 'good' or 'no good' is often determined by factors external to the solution itself, such as changing market forces, the interpretation of the

'The firms...in this report provide bespoke services for business customers with novel, complex demands.'

clients who are buying the solution, and the degree of trust that the sellers of the solution inspire. This ambiguity surrounding outcomes is central to KIFs but presents a very real barrier to measuring performance outcomes in this category of organisations. For this reason we focus on work processes (novel, complex and involving problem solution) as indicators of KIFs.

We therefore extend our definition of KIFs and describe these organisations as knowledge-intensive not only because income is generated through intangible assets but also because of *the nature of the deployment of the knowledge* held. In other words our criteria of knowledge-intensive firms extend to *the practical use of tacit knowledge in novel circumstances*. Within these criteria our research resonates with that of Lei *et al* (1999), who put renewed emphasis on the importance of innovation, initiative and competence-building in knowledge-intensive organisations. The firms that we refer to in this report provide *bespoke services for business customers with novel, complex demands*. It is within this context that tacit knowledge is the prime driver for value creation.

Industry and market characteristics

Particular industries are often referred to as knowledge-intensive – eg biotechnology or management consulting. It is, however, important to recognise that vast differences may pertain between firms within a particular industry. Large, well-known consultancies have clear and set procedures for consulting, and some of the more popular models have been presented in the management literature (Doorewaard and Meihuizen, 2000). In contrast, smaller management consultancies tend to focus on bespoke services and solutions.

We do not think it is helpful to define a particular industry as knowledge-intensive. We believe it is more important to look at the market characteristics of that industry.

Many KIFs are engaged in business-to-business relationships with a relatively small number of clients rather than selling their services directly to the end user. Supplying services to a few clients, especially when contracts are short, can create a highly unpredictable and unstable market environment. In addition, KIFs often collaborate with other similar organisations to provide services for clients. In some cases these form networks of partners which may include the clients themselves. Where they exist, such networks often require knowledge and skills to be exchanged between the various partners.

The definition of KIFs together with knowledge-intensive criteria

Drawing these points together, we define KIFs as those organisations within a knowledge economy (Drucker, 1993) that employ highly skilled individuals and therefore create market value through the application of knowledge (an intangible asset) to novel, complex client demands. These firms may work on their own or in collaboration with other similar firms.

In summary our definition of KIFs is underpinned by the firm-specific criteria:

◻ the nature and quality of their highly skilled intellectual capital

◻ the work processes which create market value through knowledge

◻ the deployment of the knowledge involving

'**One of the key characteristics that differentiates KIFs from more traditional organisations is [that] they tend to grow fast…**'

innovation, initiative and competence-building in the provision of bespoke services either independently or as part of a network of firms.

A combination of these criteria was used to guide the selection of our case studies. We present the way we went about gathering our data in these organisations next. Here we indicate how the analysis of these data links into our findings that are presented in the chapters that follow.

Research design

One of the key characteristics that differentiates a KIF from more traditional organisations is the growth pattern. These organisations have typically been born of an innovative idea that addresses a niche market need. Given the opportunity that technology affords them in terms of global marketing, they tend to grow fast – although such growth need not necessarily be in the number of people employed, for KIFs often make use of subcontractors and other alternative work arrangements. In our research, however, we focus on KIFs that are successful in the market and are faced with organic growth challenges.

It is acknowledged that KIFs encounter several growth phases (Greiner, 1998) which, in turn, enable researchers to study various organisational sizes. In our research we selected small to medium-sized organisations because we noted (through a pilot study and current literature) that KIFs at these stages of growth are faced with the most complex growth challenges. We use the European Commission's differentiation of small to medium-sized enterprises: small enterprises are those with 10 to 99 employees, and medium-sized enterprises are those with 100 to 499 employees.

Taking into account all the above KIF criteria, we selected research and technology organisations (RTOs) for study. RTOs are a recognised knowledge-intensive category (Mrinalini and Nath, 2000) and are believed to compete in terms of their knowledge intensity (ibid: 177). The basic function of RTOs is to generate knowledge to effectively enhance their clients' competitive strengths. This would imply that high-quality human capital is used to create superior client solutions in non-routinised environments.

These unique characteristics enabled us to investigate the links between people management (management of knowledge workers) and knowledge intensity (capital and nature of the work). Within the RTO category we took great care in applying the knowledge-intensive criteria to each firm, thereby acknowledging that knowledge intensity has to be evaluated on a case-by-case basis and that not all organisations in a certain category are KIFs. The application of this final criterion led us to the selection of a combination of software development and research organisations (see Figure 1 on page 10).

It is important to note that during our time of study, which was characterised by a challenging economic climate for RTOs, actually gaining access to KIFs was extremely difficult. Most organisations were interested in the research, but given acute time and cost-cutting pressures were unable to provide access. Other KIFs who were in more fortunate financial situations expressed concerns about confidentiality and presented us with their fears regarding leaks of technological and research material into the marketplace. On one occasion an organisation signed several confidentiality clauses and still refused access on the basis of growing fears about sensitive and leading-edge product information. Such challenges demonstrate KIFs' reliance on human capital and innovation for the creation of competitive advantage.

Data collection

The methodology we adopted drew on the wider People and Performance study, although important adaptations were made to cater for the distinctive characteristics of KIFs. In particular, it was not appropriate to collect data in two phases 12 months apart as we had done on the larger project – the pace of change in these organisations meant that two 'snapshots' would not give an adequate account of organisational and market challenges and changes. However, the basic principle of collecting both qualitative and quantitative data was retained.

We collected detailed data from six knowledge-intensive organisations involving a total of 221 interviews during the period October 2000 to September 2001.

Data were collected at three levels in the case organisations using two methods.

◻ Firstly, at the strategic level, semi-structured interviews were used to gain an understanding of pertinent challenges faced by the organisation, of the strategy, structure and practices within the organisation, and of how relationships with clients were being managed. These interviews were in-depth because we used them to develop an understanding of the wider context of the case company and also to identify any particular questions that needed to be asked at the operational level. The

Figure 1 | Selection of six case studies through the application of knowledge-intensive criteria

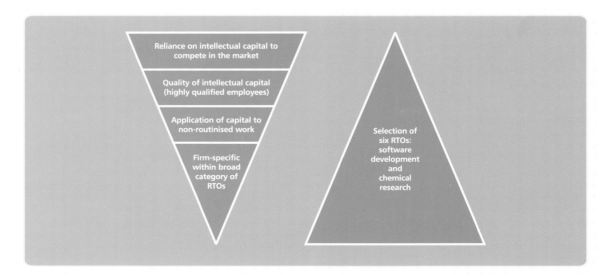

interviews varied in length from 60 to 120 minutes, and were carried out on site.

◻ Secondly, interviews were conducted at an operational level. This phase of the research was carried out in two key steps. Line managers were interviewed, using semi-structured interviews, in a specific unit of analysis that was agreed with senior managers.[1] The purpose of these interviews at operational level was to gain insight into the 'reality of the implementation of HR practices'. The line manager interviews, conducted at the KIF, lasted on average 60 minutes.

◻ Finally, further qualitative data were gathered from employees in the unit of analysis. The duration of employee interviews was typically 45 minutes, and set questions were asked about the practice of HR and also about employee attitudes. There were 118 questions asked in each interview, comprising both open-ended questions (qualitative data) and questions where a flash card was used to indicate satisfaction on scales of 1 to 4, 1 to 5, and 1 to 7. Employees were assured of confidentiality and anonymity, which facilitated

honest and elaborate answers. Our data were analysed by using a statistical package for the quantitative analysis of employee attitudes. The results were then fed back to the participating organisations as part of the research process helping us to understand the data.

In essence we followed a grounded analysis of cases (Daft and Lewin,1993: iii).

We are proposing a role for organisational scholars that is primarily one of developing new variables and theories to describe new phenomena, not to test hypotheses.

This analysis will be presented in the following chapters in thematic form, illustrating HR practices in knowledge-intensive situations. Here we also compare the characteristics of HR in practice across successful, stable and surviving KIFs.

Endnote

1   Agreement on the unit of analysis was normally reached during interviews with senior managers, and was representative of project teams who worked on specific client requests.

3 | Context and cases

The purpose of this chapter is to outline the context of our research and to present the background to the case studies. Here we focus on the context at the time of our study, in particular the decline of the 'dot.com' economy and how this influenced our case organisations. Although, as we will explain, we use a variety of measures of performance, the volatile economic environment during our study leads us to define success first and foremost as the survival of the organisation.

This research project began in October 2000 as a study of *growing* knowledge-intensive firms (GKIFs) with the specific intention of investigating the links between people management and performance in growth conditions. During this particular period the organisations in the pool that we selected for study – particularly the software development firms – were faced with severe market challenges. In late 2000 and early 2001 technology stocks plummeted, leaving many investors and venture capitalist in doubt of the value of intellectual capital.

As a financial report (BBC *News 24*, December 2000) remarked:

In the financial fairground of share dealing, there was one main attraction for London in the year 2000: the tech stocks rollercoaster. It's a ride that has one speed – white knuckle – and just two directions. Until March it was on the soar-away setting as tech stocks continued to rise on the back of the dot.com euphoria. Then came the Tech Wreck 2000, and the ride is switched into crash mode, hurling tech shares into sharp decline. By the time the year is out, leading tech stocks (as measured by the Techmark 100) will be almost a third less valuable on average than a year ago on New Year's Day 2000.

We saw the consequences of this slump in the market, otherwise known as 'the burst of the dotcom bubble', in several ways:

- Firms that agreed to participate in the research battled to grow or even maintain stable staffing levels.

- Some KIFs – especially those who were funded by venture capital – were severely negatively affected. In one month four of the organisations that we approached initially were either taken over or liquidated.

- Larger software houses (those who fall outside the small and middle-sized category) were able to take smaller firms over at very low cost, thereby decreasing competition in the market.

- The contractor employment model became less attractive as increasing numbers of highly qualified people sought permanent employment and lower payment levels were accepted. This particular consequence challenged the talent war that had been waging in KIFs.

- The combination of these factors made it increasingly difficult to maintain access to KIFs for research purposes. A key factor here was confidentiality – as the market became more aggressive and investment funds shrank, these KIFs wanted to protect cutting-edge skills and processes.

The evidence presented here is that of a general trend, and we acknowledge that some organisations triumphed amidst the market challenges and were regarded as successful. These organisations are at the heart of our study. It is

'The performance outcome that we pay attention to first and foremost is that of survival within a challenging market.'

through their *survival* that we were able to study the links between HR practices and performance.

The performance outcome that we pay attention to first and foremost is that of survival within a challenging market.

A further unique quality of our study is that we conducted our interviews (see following section) over a period of a year. In this period some of the organisations who appeared to survive initial blows from the market did suffer to a degree. Three of the KIFs found it necessary to reduce staffing levels during 2001 in order to survive in the face of increasing competition. However, one of the organisations grew phenomenally, and two remained stable.

We consider the variation in growth patterns as an opportunity to compare HR practices across different KIF conditions – ie growth, stability and staff reduction. Although we appreciate the complexity of firm performance and are not aiming to prove causality – ie HR practices that directly cause performance – this enables us to identify the *characteristics of HR practices that are associated with success in KIFs*.

We refer here specifically to the characteristics of HR practices because, unlike large organisations, these small and medium-sized KIFs seldom had HR departments or formal HR policies and did therefore not have manuals with HR policies and practices. What we did find, though, was that *the way in which people management was practised* made a critical difference to employee attitudes and behaviour.

A detailed comparison of these HR characteristics is presented in the following chapter.

The case organisations

This section describes our six organisations using a framework which draws on our methodological outline in the previous chapter:

- background – how the business originated, key services, culture, markets and competitors

- intellectual capital profile – employees, structures and processes, client relationships

- HR policies and practices – the role of HR, key HR practices, the attitude of employees toward HR practices.

The presentation of the case organisations in this chapter serves mainly as the pencil sketch of a much richer picture to be elaborated in our thematic discussion. Particular, detailed notes on the cases will be discussed in the analysis section of the report in order to link the themes that we have identified back to case material.

MPC
Background and firm performance

This small software house, located on two sites in the south-west of England, originated 16 years ago. It was the brainchild of three software engineers who wanted to focus their commercial work on bespoke software development in embedded systems. A conscious decision was made at the outset by the owners to grow their business organically and to value quality of life.

As the MD put it:

'The quality of life is the most important thing for us.'

The quality of life is the most important thing for us. You have to remember, our people are all we have. We don't have products – only people!

One of the owners was in the process of retiring, which led to the appointment of the current managing director and two other senior software engineers at director level. The organisation has managed to maintain a flat structure (only three levels: five directors, with 40 senior software engineers [SSE] and software engineers [SE]) through periods of growth. The market focus has also remained on bespoke software development, and commercial efforts are directed towards the development of modules, subcomponents and hardware-software interfaces for multinational clients.

A clear strategy is to steer away from the product route (a current trend in software development) because it is believed that this will have a devastating effect on their culture and staff retention. Their specific suite of software services means that it is difficult to recruit the right skills in the current labour market. The problem is intensified by the universities' taking a commercial approach, rather than focusing on technical specialism, in their education of software engineers.

This software house is cash-rich – it owes no funds to venture capitalists. According to the chairman it is due to its financial success that it can afford to be less traditional in its management approach. It is also successful at retaining both employees and clients – only four employees have resigned since the start of the business. Finally, the organisation occupies a dominant position within a niche market, their main competitors being independent consultants.

Firm performance during the period of the research

◻ recruitment on an ongoing basis – constant search for talent

◻ no need to reduce staff

◻ 3 per cent per year staff turnover

◻ performance bonus paid (£1,200 per employee)

◻ turnover £2,050,000, with a profit of £310,000.

Intellectual capital profile

Human capital

MPC employs 30 software engineers who specialise in systems software solutions. Our unit of analysis therefore included the whole organisation. The employees are fluent in cutting-edge languages such as ANSI C and C++, Java, Visual Basic and Delphi (to name but a few). Most of them were recruited via their university placements, thereby maintaining strong links with software education and influencing the quality of human capital upwards through the supply chain. Although most employees are software engineers, and there are only a couple of administrative staff, it would be incorrect to assume homogeneity because of specific specialist areas in software solutions. This causes software engineers to specialise in certain areas and almost to 'speak different languages', a situation in which centres of expertise then develop.

Unit of analysis

Given the nature of the workforce, the unit of analysis is the firm as a whole.

Structural capital

Sub-structures in the wider organisational structure that underpin the HR practices include:

◻ The mentoring structure involves each SSE in 'coaching' two or three protegés. None of the protegés reports to a mentor within the project structure. In other words, no employee is mentored by a SSE who is working with him or her on a project. All mentors belong to a mentoring committee which forms part of the second major organisational structure within which HR is practised.

◻ The committee structure devolves what would otherwise constitute more traditional functions, and all employees are members of at least two committees.

◻ The third 'dynamic' structure that facilitates HR practices is the project structure. This is fluid, such that an SE, an SSE or a director manages the project and employees tend to circulate between projects over time.

Client capital

This software house has a history of maintaining clients over long periods of time, so renewing contracts several times. Its key clients include Hitachi Microsystems, Psion Dacom, Sony, Varian Oncology systems and Remote Metering Systems. Client contact is not restricted to one level in the organisation, and it is a common occurrence for student software engineers to have regular contact with a client. However, one particular senior software engineer is responsible for new business development and uses the client knowledge base in the organisation to market new business.

The lengths of commercial contracts vary so that both short- and long-term projects run in parallel.

Some contracts are shorter than two man-months whereas others can exceed ten man-years. Clients include both small and large multi-national organisations and span several markets including telecommunications, retail, instrumentation and consumer electronics.

HR practices

Most HR practices are formalised,[1] in the sense that they are embedded, and the core HR roles are divided between several positions in the organisation. The business development director oversees recruitment and selection together with one other SSE. He works closely with the chief technical officer (CTO) who oversees the performance management system, which is regarded as central to other formal HR processes (skill enhancement and remuneration).

Through involvement in the mentoring committee another SSE suggested and implemented an induction programme, which has been running in this more formalised manner for the last three to four months.

The responsibility for skill enhancement rests with mentors. The directors jointly determine pay levels and make decisions about increases based on the recommendations made by the mentors as the outcome of performance appraisal discussions.

Although HR practices are formalised and the responsibility split between directors and SSE, the implementation of the HR processes is a lot more informal and the responsibility of these processes rests with mentors and project managers. Through the mentoring system the mentors, acting in a line management capacity, are responsible for the implementation of HR processes, focusing on personal and career development via the

> '...a director...may consequently be trained by a younger and more junior member of staff.'

performance management system. Project managers take a leading developmental role in a technical skill enhancement capacity. When working on a project, skills are taught by 'working together'. It should be kept in mind that a director may be reporting to an SE on a project, and may consequently be trained by a younger and more junior member of staff.

The HR architecture can therefore be presented as the relationship between HR practices (formalised with distributed responsibilities) and HR processes (informal and 'practised' by mentors and project managers). This is reflected in the presentation of the organisational structure (which reflects mentoring responsibility and sharing of cultural knowledge) alongside the project structure (which reflects technical development and houses software [skills] knowledge-sharing).

Ingenta
Background and firm performance

Ingenta is a medium-sized KIF and a world leader in e-publishing services and Web delivery in the academic and professional sector. It has substantial venture capital funding and has offices in the UK (Bath and Oxford) and the USA (Providence, RI and Boston, MA). The company started from a university computer services department in 1998, and was then commercially brought to life by its owner. Since then Ingenta has grown both organically and through acquisition – an information architecture firm (in the USA) and one competitor (a US paper-based provider of journal searches) have been acquired.

The three core services that Ingenta provide are: publisher services (online publishing platform), e-communities (creating content-rich vertical

portals) and a search facility (deep Web content). Within these three core areas its mission is to be the dominant Web intermediary for professional and academic research.

Ingenta's vision of growth is coupled with the idea of 'bigness' (as the name suggests). The company wants to create a flourishing market and occupy a dominant position in it in the shortest possible timespan. The intensive growth that Ingenta has achieved has brought with it various implications for how HR is practised in this knowledge-intensive business.

At director level the decision has been taken to integrate high technical standards with a more commercial approach, thereby combining both the services and product approaches to software development. This has led to the restructuring of the technical functions in the organisation along a project-lifecycle approach – each project has set specifications (the product approach managed by software engineers) and caters for bespoke customer requests (the services approach managed by software developers). For each project software developers work with software engineers and information architects to deliver a high-quality service and product at the lowest possible cost to the organisation.

We can only afford to retain the best employees during this phase of restructuring and cost-cutting.

Firm performance during the period of the research

◻ turnover growth of 188 per cent

◻ staff turnover of 12 per cent on average over the time of study

'The practice is for members of the executive to lead steering groups outside their area of specialism...'

- staff reduction from 255 employees in 2001 to 200 employees in 2002

- reduced use of contract workers during this period.

Intellectual capital profile

Human capital

Ingenta, as a medium-sized KIF, currently has 200 employees across a variety of specialised areas including: software engineers, software developers, sales executives, producers, project managers, information architects, visual designers, Web developers and account managers.

Our unit of analysis included the software engineers and developers that were spread over several project teams.

The majority of the employees in our unit of analysis are software engineers and developers, of whom the former concentrate on bespoke development and the latter 'build' systems that can be adapted for various customer demands. During the period of our research there was a strong move toward more standardised systems, which had a positive influence on the financial success. The human capital was negatively influenced by this development, in that employees felt that 'there was little challenge in their roles' and that 'they were not building cutting-edge skills'. This may have had an impact on the staff turnover, and consequently reduces the quality of this vital form of capital.

Structural capital

Project-team structures are most prominent in this KIF: employees from the various speciality areas working together on a specific client team. These teams tend to be very large, and several of the employees felt somewhat isolated both within their project team and from other teams in the organisation. There are opportunities for job rotation between these teams, however, although this is normally restricted to a particular job-family, and exposure to new skills is limited.

Management structures are also removed from employees. An 'executive' has been established, comprising 16 senior managers from various departmental functions. The executive is then divided further into steering groups who investigate issues such as restructuring, performance appraisal, marketing, etc. The practice is for members of the executive to lead steering groups outside their area of specialism – so that, for instance, the finance director may make suggestions on marketing plans. This practice is reckoned to 'break down barriers' and keep managers abreast of developments in departments other than their own.

Customer capital

Ingenta's clients include universities, publishers, libraries and scientific interest groups. A detailed process is followed to retain and capitalise client information. Only key members of staff deal with the client and they follow a specific process of client-contact/proposal development. This includes requirement interpretation and refining, requirement review, information architecture reports, functional specification and design management. The detailed software functions that link to the client processes are the review of the functional specifications, the building of a tailored system and the testing of this system (taken from internal documentation). Every effort is made to maintain client continuity throughout the process, thereby positioning customer capital central to the value-chain.

HR practices

Ingenta does not have a specialist HR function; HR is administered by staff that support the CFO – records of recruitment, personnel files and salary administration are housed here. The CFO views the greatest HR challenges in the face of acquisitions and growth as: the establishment of an HR database, the refinement of the employment contract, the integration of pay systems, and the implementation of the appraisal process.

In the light of these complex HR challenges to be addressed by the CFO there is heavy reliance on an external HR consultant for the formulation of HR policies, the facilitation of HR practices and the compilation of the employee handbook. The consultant has extensive contact with the organisation and works within Ingenta for a time every fortnight. During these 'visits' employees are given an opportunity to raise concerns and air grievances. A process of open consultation therefore marks the relationship between the consultant and the organisation.

In our unit of analysis the project team leaders are responsible for the day-to-day implementation of HR practices. Their roles include: recruitment needs identification and interviewing, induction, basic HR administration (records of holidays of team members) and the appraisal of performance. Each team also has a technical leader who is responsible for technical skills development. Team leaders and technical leaders give input into suggested salary increases via the remuneration committee (see below), and overall responsibility for remuneration rests with the CFO.

Our research participants felt that the maintenance of internal pay-equity was problematical due to the acquisition of organisations with differing pay systems. Although Ingenta conducted an external pay benchmarking exercise through a consultant, it was believed that 'the matching of roles' with the industry appeared to be particularly tricky due to the overall range of roles that existed within Ingenta.

Marlborough Stirling
Background and firm performance

Marlborough Stirling is a leading provider of software and services to the mortgage, life and pensions and investment market sectors. The Group delivers its software directly to clients through licensing (combined implementation, customisation and maintenance and support services). This growing and successful KIF originated in January 1987 in Cheltenham, UK, and now also has offices in Brighton, Cobham, Halesowen, Basingstoke, Dublin, Douglas in the Isle of Man, Cape Town, Madrid, Milan, Toronto and Vancouver. From the outset its focus was on the financial services industry.

Its core products include Lamda (1994), Omiga (1989) and Optimus (2000), which form part of their clients' information technology platforms that support core business processes. Lamda enables clients to manage the servicing of life, pensions, protection and investment businesses, from policy issue through to claim or maturity. Omiga facilitates the point-of-sale application processing and customer management for both regulated and non-regulated products. Optimus manages mortgage business from the release of funds through to redemption, including comprehensive borrower retention and securitisation capabilities. Their clients include Alliance&Leicester, Bank of Scotland, Clerical Medical, Egg, Nationwide Building Society, Sanlam and Sun Life Financial of Canada.

'Flexibility ...necessitates constant research and development.'

At the start of our research Marlborough Stirling (UK) was categorised as a medium-sized company (504 employees) but by mid-2001 this number had increased to 840 employees worldwide. The chairman attributes this growth to 'the quality of our people, software and track record'. The business has grown organically and through acquisition, which has enabled a wider geographical coverage. Establishing joint ventures with some of its clients enabled further growth.

Our focus on people makes us profitable, and this is driven right from the top by the chairman.

These diverse client-relationship arrangements are reflected in the suite of products as well as the manner in which they are offered. A combination of insourcing, outsourcing, third-party administration (TPA), managed services and application service provision are made available. Some of the services are sold to clients without support; others are accompanied by continuous support. Often third-party administration is offered by which the KIF's own systems will be used on its own site to administer its clients' life and pension business/mortgage books.

As the marketing director remarked:

You cannot have only one solution for several companies.

This flexibility with services and products accounts further for the success of the company. It is important to mention here that the flexibility – which is at the heart of the product suite – necessitates constant research and development. This aspect enables software developers to constantly update skills and ensures that the work is not routinised (see KIF criteria, Chapter 2).

At the start of our research this firm was privately owned. During mid-2001, however, Marlborough Stirling announced its intention to float on the stock market, and did so effectively. This enabled further successful growth but held several implications for cultural change and people management. Several of our research participants remarked that it enabled the company to grow too fast and in such a way that there was almost a misfit between the growth and the company culture – 'a growing company with a small-company mentality'.

Firm performance during the time of the research

- turnover[2] £50.1 million

- 4 per cent of turnover came from overseas contracts

- turnover grew by 58 per cent per annum between 1998 and 2000.

Intellectual capital

Human capital
Given the size of this KIF and its client base, it has employees in a variety of specialist areas – software developers, internal IT support, administration and corporate services.[3] The majority of the employees are software developers and write codes to enable the sale of both products and services. These employees all have qualifications in software development and are often recruited from the local area.

Marlborough Stirling has also taken care to influence the content of software development courses provided at local educational establishments, thereby influencing human capital upwards through the supply chain.

In our study we focused on the software engineers who work both for clients and within the organisation, developing software for client work that is conducted on the premises of the KIF. The majority of the staff are younger than 29 and male. One third of the employees were new to their jobs (in their current position for less than a year).

Our unit of analysis was software developers in Lamda, Omiga and internal technology services.

Structural capital

The KIF is organised in a traditional manner according to functional specialisms – ie finance, HR, legal, sales and marketing, training ('the Academy'), delivery, and research and development. These traditional functions are used as support mechanisms for the products, Lamda, Omiga and Optimus. Software developers are grouped into these product/project teams. Given the relatively few teams for the size of the company, project teams tend to be large and there is little communication between the traditional functions and the teams. Some participants referred to a 'silo mentality' and felt that boundaries were clear.

The management structure comprises a main board, an operational board and an operational executive. The operational executive has influence over day-to-day activities and is influential in making key strategic decisions. Line managers, team managers and project managers sit in this group. Its composition enables the operational executive to act as a link between employees and management.

Customer capital

Marlborough Stirling takes great care in nurturing client relationships. It has entered into joint ventures with clients and its several external partnerships include:

◘ participation in the '. net' group – one of the first companies in the world to work with Microsoft

◘ informal relationships with companies regarded as influencers in the industry. Here market knowledge is shared, company developments briefed and mutual opportunities discussed. The influencer and the KIF often have common clients and may be in competition from time to time. Particular examples are:

◘ consulting actuaries (the KIF keeps them aware of developments)

◘ large management consultancies: 'We provide solutions for their clients'

◘ reinsurance companies, who list the KIF as a preferred supplier.

HR practices

This KIF has an HR and a training and development department, known in combination together as 'the Academy'. The Academy and HR functions work separately, however. The Academy focuses on the development of organisational development strategies. HR is responsible for HR operations, recruitment, internal communication, health and safety, and pay and benefits. A team of 25 staff reports to the head of group HR, who has seen the company grow from 180 employees to its current

> '…the head of group HR regarded on-the-job training as one of the most effective ways of learning in this knowledge-intensive environment.'

size. This composition ensures that people management issues are addressed at this strategic level in the organisation.

Recruitment of new staff is conducted in a partnership with line management. A recruitment officer is assigned to a vacancy and advises line management of appropriate procedures to fill the position. Standard recruitment campaigns run throughout the year (website and local press) and the orientation is toward constant recruitment of the 'talent that comes along'. During the recruitment process use is made of in-house technical tests and personality tests. Large numbers of employees are often recruited by means of a single recruitment drive.

Training and development is delivered by the Academy, which runs both induction training and skills training. The practice is that training programmes follow a performance appraisal during which training needs are identified. The performance appraisal is based on identifying objectives, which are then agreed between the line manager and the employee. The annual appraisal is documented and comprises a review of the objectives for the previous year, a summary of performance through the year in relation to those objectives, and the setting of objectives for the following year. It is through reference to this performance history as well as to future career objectives that training needs are identified. An interim review is also held to discuss career aspirations and to update the company's skills matrix.

Formal training is also complemented by informal guidance and coaching. Indeed, the head of group HR regarded on-the-job training as one of the most effective ways of learning in this knowledge-intensive environment. That environment is emphasised in Marlborough Stirling, and coaching is seen as a central part of management. Coaching skills are also delivered as part of the Academy's suite of programmes.

Marlborough Stirling believes that its salaries and benefits packages compare favourably with other employers' in the local area. Individual salaries are linked to individual performance and market rates. Information on market rates is translated into salary bands which are attached to all Marlborough Stirling job roles.

Marlborough Stirling has established a salary and benefits review board to review salary and benefits on an ongoing basis, in order to ensure that the company's reward policies are appropriate and applied consistently. The operational executive (senior management team) is regularly asked for input into these reviews. Management positions are assessed against business objectives, and managers can earn up to 5 per cent of their bonus through performance.

Microgen-Kaisha
Background and firm performance

Microgen-Kaisha is part of a larger plc known as the Microgen Group, comprising billing and database management, software consulting (Kaisha) and e-payment (Telesmart). The billing and database management division derived from the original business operations and generates recurring revenue from transactional activities of billing, payment and online database management services. Telesmart was acquired in August 2000 in order to provide payment solutions to the business-to-business (B_2B) sector (payment software, consultancy and e-payment services).

Microgen-Kaisha (once an independent operation) was acquired by the Microgen Group in April 1999 to focus on information management solutions, client relationship management, knowledge management and e-business systems within sectors compatible with the transactional services operation. Because all day-to-day operational decisions were decentralised and people management decisions were being made at divisional level, we investigated Microgen-Kaisha only – a restriction on our selection imposed by the knowledge-intensive criteria that we set at the start of the research. The discussion that follows is therefore mainly applicable to the consulting arm of the business (Microgen-Kaisha).

This KIF employs approximately 75 consultants as well as 35 client support service staff, and is based on one site in the south-west of the UK.[4] Its focus is on the provision of consultancy advice that addresses all aspects of information management, including the design, implementation and subsequent support of individual IT systems. As a software consultancy it prides itself on the ability to take a holistic view of IT solutions, and addresses the interface between the client's business and the technological solution. In this context, knowledge management services are defined as the systematic collection, storage and distribution of information within an organisation to improve company performance (Kaisha internal document, 2001). The design and delivery of solutions as well as the hosting and maintenance of systems are all individually tailored to clients' requirements. Key principal consultants who spend extensive periods of time at the client's premises facilitate the bespoke nature of this work.

Firm performance during the period of the research

◘ operating margin before Group overhead increased to 25 per cent

◘ financial turnover growth was 10 per cent

◘ annual revenue was £8.8 million

◘ operating profit was £2.2 million

◘ annual staff turnover was 13 per cent; according to a company director this is

not high enough to ensure a continual refresh of the skills and approaches required by an IT company.

Intellectual capital profile

Human capital
The 110 employees are culturally and structurally divided into two categories: fee-earners and non-fee-earners. As the managing director stated: 'We are on a fee-earning treadmill' where actions are constantly equated to money earned.

Most fee-earners are experienced consultants who have worked in many other organisations, and a number have been self-employed IT consultants. The consultants are divided further into grades 4–7 on the company job-grading system: grades 4–5 focus on technical work and most of the software development, grades 5–6 relate to business systems analysis and some development, while grade 7 is that of the principal consultants who

> 'A project team typically consists of a project manager, business analysts and technical consultants.'

are project managers or technical architects. The latter category is regarded as including the most experienced employees in the organisation, who are heavily involved in the development of employees at the other grade levels.

Unit of analysis

Our unit of analysis included software consultants across levels 4–7 who were working on various client projects on the premises of the KIF, as well as software support staff who were developing and maintaining both client and internal systems.

A senior director who has championed many 'women in IT' campaigns was eager to establish an equal balance between female and male employees. This workforce is somewhat different from the other KIFs in respect of the age and gender split of the human capital profile.

Our data also evidenced the presence of 'careerists' who were eager to move ahead and who had both their own interest and the organisation's success in mind.

In this business and current climate, the average time you can hope to keep a consultant is two years – anything more than that is a bonus.

This notion was in stark contrast with support staff, who by definition were also knowledge workers (programming and developing software) but who preferred 'not to be out on the road all the time'. These employees sought a work–life balance and felt that the fee-earning measures – such as utilisation targets of 75 per cent – were often not appreciative of the support staff's role.

Structural capital
The Microgen Group plc has nine executive directors who report directly to the chairman –

three of these directors are within the Kaisha structure. There is representation for HR at the board level through the company secretary, who is responsible on a Group-wide basis for HR. Beyond the director level the structure is flat, involving only four levels of consultants. A few support staff (finance, HR and operations analysis) report directly to the managing director of Microgen-Kaisha.

Undoubtedly, the most prominent structure is the project team: it is within this team that client concerns are managed and fees earned.

A project team typically consists of a project manager, business analysts and technical consultants. The business development manager may involve technical staff when pitching for business. This enables the client to understand the technical detail of the system. Once the proposal has been written and reaches a 90 per cent probability of acceptance, the consultancy manager will assign sufficient resources to the project team and a project manager will be appointed. The size of the teams varies according to client demands, but can involve between four and 20 staff members.

A team will also evolve over time, as software consultants will exit after completing their 'share of the work'. This might be difficult to manage because new staff may have to be introduced to a team already familiar with client specifications. However, the development of skills is addressed by this continuous circulation between teams, which is central to staff retention in this 'competitive' environment.

Client capital
Client contact often originates from business in the other operational areas of Microgen, thereby

indicating that client information is frequently shared in order to increase total KIF market share. Client contact is mainly maintained and developed by a single business development manager and the marketing manager who reports to that position. This KIF is renowned for getting repeat business from current clients, and presents this fact proudly in glossy brochures and also in their offices. Some key clients include British Gas, Allied Domecq, WH Smith, Daewoo, and ICI.

Microgen-Kaisha offered the flexibility, support advice and the people we needed when we needed them … Four years later they are still working with us.
        (client quote from company documentation)

HR practices

Given the current economic downturn, Microgen-Kaisha has decided only to replace attrition.

The knowledge-intensity of the skills needed in the business was emphasised by both management and employees. Unlike our other case organisations, this led to the formalisation of the recruitment process because this process was seen to be critical in getting the right skills in. A major selection criterion was the ability to cope with change. This was important because of the constant change experienced in project-based teams.

The use of contract workers was introduced to complement the skills within the project team. As a project manager commented:

We bring contractors in if we do not have the skills internally, and also if we aren't going to need them on a constant basis. We do not use contractors on a long-term basis. If it is a very specific skill that is

needed on a project, which we feel may be of use in the future, we will get a bright young consultant to work with the contractor in order to pick up the skill. This is how we create our experts.

The HR process considered to be key in the retention and development of staff is the performance appraisal process. Performance data is gathered by performance reviewers, who might be senior and principal consultants. These are then assigned by the consultancy manager to review the performance of employees that fit their employment profile. Main sources of performance data include the project managers, peers on a project, and the client. Data are gathered after each project or every three months (on long projects). All data are sent to (and gathered by) reviewers, who then compile a performance review summary.

Performance reviews are conducted every three months. One review is more formal, at which the employee undertakes self-assessment and discusses and compares the 360-degree review. The outcome is recorded, and development needs and future goals are set jointly. The employee will also be scored on a five-point scale, and these scores are taken into account when the yearly bonus is calculated for payment.

No formal training processes were in place and development was mainly achieved on an informal basis during project work. Here the focus was mainly on the transfer of skills through the resource allocation process (getting people with different areas of specialism to work on the same project). The on-the-job learning process was also not formalised – the extent of skill development provision given to junior staff was at the discretion of the project manager.

'The issue of pay and reward therefore appears to be very much a top-down process.'

No mention was made of involvement in decision-making processes, and it appears that teamworking is the main vehicle for involvement. The managing director did speak briefly about discussion forums that were set up but not used, the newsletter that receives little or no input or attention. It seems as if there is very little interest from the employees in looking inward into the organisation and taking part in organisational activities.

No one knows how the pay level is specified – I only know my own pay, and I'm not sure about internal equity.

The salary structure comprises a basic salary, car allowance for fee-earners and client-facing employees, business and private fuel card, discretionary share options, a profit-sharing bonus and 7 per cent pension contributions, as well as private health. Directors in the organisation control internal equity by comparing the pay rates for the various positions. Line managers and project managers make recommendations to the senior managers of the division regarding pay increases, and feedback regarding their acceptance comes back from the board. The issue of pay and reward therefore appears to be very much a top-down process.

Performance bonuses are also paid on the outcome of the appraisal process, and exceptional performance is rewarded through an employee-of-the-month scheme. Employees are enthusiastic about this scheme and commented that it recognised their input.

Tocris Cookson
Background and firm performance

This small research firm adheres to the knowledge-intensive criteria that we used to select the cases that have been presented – but unlike our other case organisations it is not a software or Web-development firm. Tocris Cookson, which has 60 employees, is a specialist chemical company with experience in the synthesis of a wide variety of compounds that often contain complex biologically active molecules. This KIF employs teams of skilled chemists (mainly at post-doctoral level) and operates from one site in the UK and one site in the USA.

In addition to the production of catalogue compounds for the life sciences, Tocris Cookson offers custom synthesis and contract research services. This part of the business is particularly challenging and novel. The catalogue chemists argued strongly that catalogue work involved the same degree of novelty as custom synthesis. The reason for this was that methods published in academic texts were frequently difficult to follow, and even if a compound was not entirely new, the procedure might well be.

Tocris Cookson originated in 1994 from a merger between Cookson Chemicals – a Southampton-based research company – and Tocris, a Bristol-based life science research outfit. Both these organisations were started by research chemists within university chemistry departments when a key scientist noticed a commercial opportunity to produce chemical compounds. In order to integrate the two businesses Tocris Cookson bought new premises in Bristol (UK) and built state-of-the-art laboratories. All UK employees work from this site, and compounds are dispatched internationally.

Before the new Bristol site was opened, Tocris Cookson started a micro-venture in St Louis (USA). This was inaugurated as a response to delays experienced in getting chemicals past customs, whereupon it was decided that a US-based site would facilitate getting the compounds to the clients as fast as their American competitors could.

The business is cash-rich: no funds are owed to venture capitalists. Indeed, the directors feel that they may have been too cautious in investment and spending. It continues to recruit and work closely with universities in order to identify suitable talent. Unlike our other firms, Tocris Cookson did not experience the same economical downturn and was looking to expand further at the time we completed our research.

Firm performance during the period of the research

◘ sales targets exceeded by 33 per cent

◘ financial turnover growth was £3,583,000– £4,964,000

◘ operating profit was £474,000–£910, 000

◘ staff turnover involved six employees (9.4 per cent).

Intellectual capital profile

All our experience is home-grown.

Human capital

Most employees are recruited during a post-doctoral placement at the company. This is often their first full-time employment. It is a situation that is regarded as a potential danger by the management of the company because the majority of their workforce is young, highly qualified and mobile. The threat is managed by means of a strong organisational culture, which employees describe as that of a family or a home-from-home. Given that most employees join the organisation straight from university and that strong university ties are maintained in order to develop skills and attract suitable employees, this KIF has a very distinctive 'university' feel to it.

The majority of the 60 employees have a chemistry PhD, and it is they who conduct all the syntheses. They are supported by staff in the packing and weighing room who weigh and dispatch orders to clients. Other business support services include finance, business development, client services and facilities management.

Unit of analysis

In the light of the size of the organisation and the intricate links between the various functions, we interviewed all employees in this KIF.

Structural capital

This KIF is largely organised around the production of compounds: the key structural groupings are the catalogue and custom synthesis research teams. The teams are divided further into radiochemistry and chemistry. In both these groups compounds are made at 'bays' in a laboratory. A bay is a workbench with equipment that is large enough to accommodate four chemists. Our interviews indicated that these four chemists would then be identified as a team, yet

> 'There appeared to be a divide between the chemistry and support divisions both structurally and socially.'

the team boundaries appeared to be unclear, and during our visits to the company complex conversations were normally held across bays.

Because of the similar age and background of the research chemists, they would normally engage in lively debates over lunch, gather socially after work and describe themselves as colleagues and friends. It was as if this 'social structure' was as evident at work as it was outside work hours.

Some of the chemists were selected to be managers, yet within the KIF structure they appeared to be in a position similar to that of the research chemists. The managers felt that their positions were no different (they were still making chemicals) but that their roles were stretched – they dedicated 20 per cent of their time to being people managers. The key tasks here were the development of other research chemists who might not be part of their team and conducting performance appraisals.

Another key structural part of the organisation is the support services – the packing and weighing room and the business support services such as finance, business development and client services. There appeared to be a divide between the chemistry and support divisions both structurally (as portrayed on charts) and socially. Attempts were made to integrate these two divisions by setting up discussion forums. Such forums were intended to comprise both chemistry and support services employees, and their purpose was to address a central business issue – eg client relationships. Although this might appear useful, it seemed to have little value to the overall business and the forums were described to us as 'toothless'.

Client capital

Tocris Cookson's key clients are life science researchers at universities or other research institutes. In order to build these clients' relationships and, indeed, make the compounds, this KIF has to maintain very strong ties with large pharmaceutical companies, patent lawyers and academics in the field. The reason for this is that pharmaceutical firms often have patents on some of the chemicals that must be synthesised, although the patents may well lapse after an 8- to 10-year period. If a 'cool chemical is spotted', the patent rights must then be negotiated with the relevant firm. A senior manager in Tocris Cookson believed that these relationships, which are developed over years, are central to the company's success.

Relationships with universities must also be maintained, for three particular reasons:

◘ to update employees' skills in the pharmacological discipline

◘ to build client relationships in situations where the universities are often users of the compounds made

◘ to build an external recruitment pool by making top-performing research chemists aware of the business.

Our interviews suggested that the process of building client capital was an 'art' and could be mastered only over several years of experience, first as a doctoral chemist, then as a post-doctoral researcher, and finally as a negotiator with major pharmaceutical firms.

HR practices

Most formalised HR practices originated from an elaborate HR policy, which was written by the part-time HR manager. She joined the organisation three years prior to our research after she became consultant to Tocris Cookson on employee-related matters. During our interviews we seemed to hear two versions of HR practices: those prescribed in the employee handbook, and those practised on a day-to-day basis by the employees and managers.

The HR manager listed her key responsibilities as: setting up a database/record of employee skills, setting up policies, procedures and the employee handbook (outlining clearly what should be done and when), writing policies that focus on performance appraisal, management development and strategic management, and helping directors to delegate responsibility.

For all concerned, the most important set of practices were those that were related to the performance appraisal. Two appraisal systems are in operation – chemists have a set of competencies separate from the support staff's and therefore a separate system of appraisal. This is because it is very difficult to appraise the outcome of research. Some argue that a top researcher might spend a considerable length of time working on a new compound and may even then have no immediate output to show, and yet when the compound is eventually put into production it may prove to be very valuable to the business. A negative appraisal before the compound is completed may cost the business thousands of pounds. A focus purely on input is not desirable either, however, because hours spent in the lab do not necessarily equate to good work.

The new appraisal system is based on *competencies* (technical and generic), which are then categorised by specific descriptors into specific *bands*, and all staff are appraised according to this system *on a 360-degree basis*.

For support staff appraisals take place every six months: in April the focus is on pay, and in October it is on development. Chemists have one annual and three interim reviews, based on a system that they have developed themselves.

The best I can describe it is [as] a process of discovery: I am not sure what it is to be used for and how often we should do it. The appraisal process has also been evolving over the last three years.

The process has changed a lot. It used to be a lot clearer when it was related to pay – now it is a case of looking on a checklist and seeing if performance is on a desired level.

According to this system a role is broken down into eight competency bands, and descriptors are set for each competency on each band. Individuals' scores are given against descriptors for the relevant band. Objectives are then set and development paths identified for an individual to progress through bands. The objectives are set jointly during the performance appraisal process. Chemists are given an opportunity to disagree and make their own input into what is decided for the next period of appraisal. Points in the bands are linked to salary points, although the general belief is that there is no clear link between appraisal and pay.

The development programmes linked to the appraisal process were in a stage of infancy at the time of our research. Most skills development took place on an informal basis after a manager 'gathered' that a certain employee needed to develop a particular skill. Tocris Cookson provided classic examples of 'learning from the master' and workplace learning. Training was also described as employee-driven, although it was a formal practice

> **'...a mentor is assigned to each new employee, who will then work very closely with the mentor for up to one year.'**

to train every employee for some three to four days per year and there was additionally a training budget set aside for chemistry conferences and the funding of further degrees, such as the MBA.

If there is a new, inexperienced employee, we will seat an experienced chemist next to the employee in the lab. We take mentoring very seriously.

Supervisory courses had just been started for employees in leadership roles, and everyone in a client-facing role was attending presentation skills courses. Methods of training that were used included:

◻ in-house training in small teams by a team leader

◻ one-day training seminars given by external consultants brought onto the site

◻ seminars and lectures from other outside experts.

A formalised mentoring system was also in place to enhance skills development, although this appeared to operate mainly in the chemistry division. Within this system a mentor is assigned to each new employee, who will then work very closely with the mentor for up to one year. It was felt that in respect of a lot of the coaching given the academic culture encouraged employees to regard it as important to have the opportunity to learn from more experienced staff. Furthermore,

the nature of the knowledge is very complex and cannot be passed down easily.

Finally, the structure and layout (teachers and learners were physically located together) enhanced knowledge-sharing and learning.

Academic answers to 'learning questions' will never give you the edge – you can't do it without it, but it would not give you the edge.

Integration into the way of working through experienced chemists – this is how they get used to the 'ways of the company'. That is why we recruit straight out of academia and grow the commercial experience here.

Previously, the issue of pay was always kept very much behind closed doors. The managing director would interview all employees and then decide on a percentage increase for each employee. No one knew whether it was market-related or not. Great efforts have been made to improve this situation by reviewing the market-relatedness of the base pay (through surveys) and formalising the increase system. At the time of our research, an external firm had just completed surveys, and every person's salary was benchmarked against similar jobs in the industry. After salaries were adjusted to the median, specific bands were developed. This appears to be a broadbanding approach in which particular skills (training) and competencies (performance levels) are attached to each band.

This way, employees know exactly what they need to do to increase their pay levels – which provides a great motivational force. For the first time there are clear links between performance and pay.

The salary structure comprises basic pay (benchmarked and broadbanded), a performance bonus (related to company performance), and a four per cent contribution to a personal pension fund selected by the firm.

Other methods of reward include the Tocris Cookson OSCA (outstanding skill contribution achievement), which was suggested by a member of staff and is a system by which people are rewarded for doing something extra (not necessarily business-related, eg organising the Christmas meal). A reward of £25 is given to the employee.

Team recognition is given in the form of taking a team out to dinner if a job has been well done or has finished on time. Individual token rewards are also given for outstanding performance.

Most employees were satisfied with the reward process and felt that it contributed to their motivation. The strongest intrinsic motivation, however, was in relation to a reward specifically linked to doing a good job as a chemist.

Epinet Communications Plc
Background and firm performance

We had the opportunity to study a very interesting phase of this small KIF at the start of our research. Epinet had just merged with Gatley Hall & Co, bringing consulting experience together with software development. Both these organisations were approximately 10 years old at the time of the merger, and had to face several integration challenges. The professional services director described these phases as:

the physical move, organisational restructuring, performance management, and strategic planning phases.

The two cultures of the counterparts to the merger were very different. Gatley Hall focused on organisational development and knowledge management consulting, employing a small professional team, and Epinet was described as a 'techie firm' with a young workforce. Both KIFs

were situated on a working dairy farm in the Cotswolds, and it was a shared vision for growth as well as a shared location that facilitated the merger.

Epinet – the larger of the two firms – generated revenue through bespoke application service provision: 40 per cent of its income came from the automotive markets, 25 per cent from health care, and 25 per cent from trade and education (as detailed in their business plan and quarterly reports). Pooling the talent from both organisations, Epinet Plc aimed to provide clients with holistic and bespoke technology solutions. In other words, both consultants and software experts would work together to develop applications and address wider organisational impacts of the implementation of the new technology – ie cultural, structural and strategy matters.

It was difficult to ascertain exactly which sectors this new business would be targeting because at the time of our interviews Epinet was in the process of adjusting to the merger and addressing differences in management style and strategic vision.

Firm performance during the period of the research

◘ turnover increased from £1.2 million (2000) to £1.4 million

◘ profitability: a small loss was incurred

◘ the professional consultancy de-merged from software development

◘ staff numbers decreased from 30 to 25.

'...there is little formality to the structure – what is shown on the organisational chart is irrelevant to how people actually interact.'

Intellectual capital profile

Human capital
At the time of the research, Epinet employed 30 staff – four consultants (covering both management development and technological consulting), five support staff (administration, finance and staff management), 12 software developers, three project managers and six sales and marketing staff.

This small KIF competes within a very tight labour market for talent: it draws from the same labour pool as Marlborough Stirling (see above). Many software developers also prefer to work for better-known organisations in order to develop their own careers. Despite the exceptionally pleasant working conditions (a renovated barn in the Cotswolds), recruitment presents some challenges because of the competition within the local labour market.

Various rivals (of similar size) can offer some of the same services at a more competitive rate because they employ software developers in countries where labour is considerably less expensive. In response, Epinet recruits employees from similar countries but supplies them with working permits and accommodation in the United Kingdom. Both the employees and the managing director believed that this was a successful strategy because it created a family atmosphere and demonstrated concern for the employees' welfare.

Unit of analysis
The unit of analysis included both software developers and consultants.

Structural capital
Unlike other small KIFs who have a fairly homogeneous workforce, Epinet has a considerably well-staffed support structure akin to larger and more traditional organisations. More than 25 per cent of the employees are not software developers or consultants. The support structures are also hierarchical and more traditional. There are several layers. (One layer comprises a technical architect, a production manager responsible for managing the scheduling of work, and a senior project manager. Other layers include programmers, designers and project managers, and there is a layer for a junior programmer position available to a school-leaver.) The layers together contribute to a number of divisions, each made up of 12 employees.

Closer inspection of 'how the structure works in practice', however, gives an indication that there is little formality to the structure – what is shown on the organisational chart is irrelevant to how people actually interact.

The informal picture is somewhat different. The barn has several 'play rooms' where software developers can relax, talk about coding issues or 'just hang out'. For example, the latest version of PlayStation had just been installed in one of the rooms – so this is where 'games were played' ... and also where many software problems were solved. The existence of the play rooms was intended to encourage developers to feel free to leave their workstations and also because, although playing games at the workstation was not banned, it was not encouraged. Such informal interaction appeared to be at the heart of skills development and knowledge-intensive work.

Client capital
The development of client capital seemed as informal as the structure of the organisation. It appeared that long-term relationships with clients were maintained and that clients were also treated as 'friends and family'. The relatively large number

of employees in the new marketing department were in the process of accumulating client capital through previous work experience and both national and international contacts. There was some evidence of recorded client information found on the intranet – eg client contact details and a project management space in which project details were recorded and development and project management time logged. But there appeared to be no client procedures or guidance on how to interpret a client specification, as seen in our other organisations. It would seem that following up informal introductions and opportunities played a large part in winning business and getting new leads.

HR practices

Epinet does not have a dedicated HR department and the informal role of 'looking after people management' rests with the Group services director. This aside, the team leaders in the software development teams were serious about people management, and meetings were often held to discuss either recruitment or development issues. One particular team leader arranged several seminars that addressed contemporary software issues, and also circulated reading material to his team and other interested parties.

Recruitment was known to be extremely *ad hoc* in this KIF. Many enlightening stories were told of how software developers came to join the organisation. For example, the managing director once met someone at an airport while in transit, and the meeting turned into an interview that led to a job offer before the plane was boarded. Somehow the informality and the 'value of the moment' has enabled Epinet to find high-quality staff who are loyal to the company.

The only formalised process was the performance appraisals, regarded as a personal developmental and skills tool rather than as an indicator towards a percentage pay increase. All team leaders were trained in the use of the appraisal, and all staff attended a workshop on what to expect from an appraisal. Formal performance discussions were held at the start of the calendar year and included a review of pay. Two areas of performance were reviewed:

◻ general areas – creativity and innovation, client management, self-management, people skills and leadership

◻ role-specific areas – these are agreed with the team leader, and behavioural examples are used as evidence of a certain level of performance.

A motivation plan (drawn up from internal documentation) is completed at the end of the review to encourage performance improvement through development.

No formal training and development processes are in place – the emphasis is on employee-driven informal development. If employees identify external courses that would be useful for skills development, the KIF may fund them. If an employee then leaves within the first year, he or she is contractually obliged to repay the training money. The director responsible for the employee decides whether the particular course is relevant. A training budget of 3 per cent of turnover is set aside for developmental purposes.

Pay is a very subjective issue. There is no objective structure and clarity … it also feels that my effort is not reflected in my pay.

The pay structure used in Epinet is mainly skills-based, which for software developers translates into:

the more and the latest programming languages you are familiar with, the more you get paid.

There is some flexibility in this structure, though, based on experience and international exposure. The reward packages did not compare well on average with other local competitors' – no additional benefits were offered (no flexi-time, no pension and shorter holidays). The informality of the recruitment process also meant that there was a lack of internal pay equity because different terms and conditions were agreed at the recruitment stage.

In the majority of the interviews it was clear that the performance of the employees is driven by:

◘ personal pride in their work

◘ a sense of ownership of the projects

◘ the feeling that they can influence the way of working in the company, that they can make a difference.

I am willing to sacrifice some money for a better quality of life ... the location and more influence in a smaller company ... Here I'm able to make a difference.

Endnotes

1 The processes of formalisation take place through the committee structure, by which suggestions from directors, SSE and SE are published on the intranet, discussed at a formal gathering, and approved by directors at their monthly meeting.

2 Turnover is generated primarily from licence, customisation and implementation fees, maintenance and support services and outsourcing services.

3 Corporate services include finance, HR, legal, sales and marketing.

4 The Group operation is somewhat larger, spread across four sites in England and Wales.

4 | Identifying knowledge-intensive situations

We have discussed the ways in which knowledge can create a competitive advantage in general terms. Before we can make progress with the analysis, however, we should pinpoint the ways in which knowledge creates value in more practical terms. In particular, we must understand what it is about the way certain firms manage their knowledge that is associated with improved performance. In short – what are the knowledge-intensive processes and situations that are critical to the success of the business?

This chapter therefore endeavours to identify the knowledge-intensive situations that must be managed well to improve the performance of the business, while the following chapter looks at the people management practices which contribute to the management of these situations.

In order to do this we have to ask:

◘ How does knowledge flow in these organisations?

◘ Which knowledge processes are present in all our case organisations?

◘ Which knowledge-intensive situations are considered to create a competitive advantage?

Our definition of knowledge-intensive situations includes the creation and development of tacit skills, the sharing, through practice, of know-how, and the embedding of knowledge into organisational routines and practices.

> **A definition of knowledge-intensive situations**
>
> A knowledge-intensive situation occurs where the flow of knowledge can create a competitive advantage, and where the possession of knowledge is therefore considered a core competence.

The three main knowledge-intensive situations that we discuss here are:

◘ the enhancement of knowledge creation and knowledge flow through learning-by-doing: the focal point is the *knowledge worker and the project* or knowledge-intensive work itself

◘ knowledge-sharing within an organisation where the quality of boundaries influences the knowledge-sharing process – this focuses on knowledge flow through practice and conversation *between the knowledge worker and the team* and *between teams*

◘ knowledge-sharing between the organisation, its partners (if they exist) and the client where again the quality of boundaries influences the knowledge-sharing process – this focuses on knowledge flow through practice and conversation *between the organisation and its clients and any network members.*

'...knowledge creation starts with an investment in tacit knowledge.'

Knowledge creation through learning-by-doing

Most knowledge workers agree that knowledge-intensive work starts by 'figuring things out by yourself', 'trying different paths to a solution', and 'learning from your own mistakes'. This indicates that prior to knowledge-sharing a great deal of knowledge creation takes place on an individual level at which each knowledge worker engages with and in knowledge work.

Nonaka and Takeuchi (1995) in their seminal text *The Knowledge Creating Company* alluded to the fact that knowledge creation starts with an investment in tacit knowledge. Here learning takes place through doing, active engagement/practice and reflection, and asking questions about practice. This is also they key process that builds human capital – it is through tacit skill accumulation that the human capital is strengthened within the organisation. According to knowledge-based theory, the development of tacit skill is the first step in the knowledge-creating spiral by which tacit skill is shared through practice, then formalised through organisational routines which serves as a context within which new employees acquire these organisation-specific tacit skills (see Figure 2).

The knowledge spiral indicates that collective knowledge-sharing originates at individual level, within the act of solving problems and learning. Although this could be true for many organisations, our KIFs actively invested time in these knowledge processes. The notion of

Figure 2 | The knowledge-creating spiral with tacit skill accumulation as its focus (adapted from Nonaka and Takeuchi, 1995)

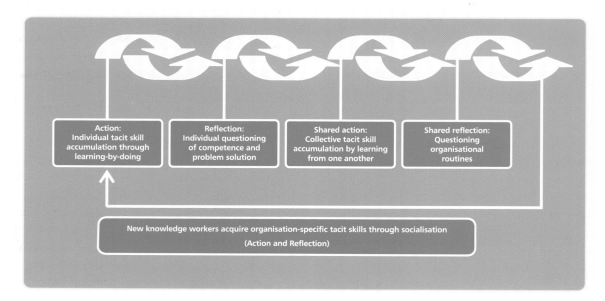

'A core part of our interviewing methodology at both line manager and employee level was the exploration of knowledge-sharing processes...'

continuous learning was driven by the organisational culture and actively enacted through what knowledge workers did every day. It was part of the 'way of thinking' in the successful KIFs. Employees were given redundant time[1] to develop new software development skills by 'messing about on the Internet', 'trying new things to see how it worked' or trying 'different solutions to current client work' in order to develop individual tacit skills:

We learn mainly on the job, but we have to support each other and learn from each other as well.

(respondent at Microgen Kaisha)

Tacit skill accumulation at individual level through learning-by-doing was also supported by such measures as a formalised mentoring system and performance management systems. Both these types of system were used to encourage learning and to enforce the behavioural norms in the organisation. This is where the collective tacit skill accumulation cuts across the individual level of learning: it is important to learn new software code/methods of synthesis but it will only be valuable to the organisation if the new skills are applied to projects in the organisation and become specific to the organisation, thereby creating a competitive advantage.

A knowledge worker who uses redundant time to acquire valuable skills must apply this skill to the writing of software which then translates into chargeable action. This skill must be shared with other software engineers in order to give the organisation as a whole an advantage over its competitors. Likewise, a student engineer who has cutting-edge technical knowledge must learn organisation-specific ways of skill application before that knowledge can be translated into

intellectual capital in knowledge-intensive processes.

The focal point of learning individually through reflection on the project or acquiring organisation-specific skills through observing others is that the behavioural dimensions of the skills cannot be verbalised. Several knowledge workers and research chemists emphasised the fact that only experience can serve as a foundation for competence. It was through the application of technical knowledge that an individual and other knowledge workers around the individual would learn.

Taught training courses were therefore of little value – it was only the sharing of experience in different communities within the organisation and with the client that laid a solid foundation for knowledge creation. Participants commented that 'you could not tell someone how to do something but it was through doing things together that you could learn more'. Nonetheless, conversations were considered to be an important aspect of knowledge processes – but they were embedded in shared practice where the expounded knowledge was built upon shared tacit meanings.

Knowledge-sharing within organisations

A core part of our interviewing methodology at both line manager and employee level was the exploration of knowledge-sharing processes: 13 questions over 221 interviews. We asked specific questions about how knowledge is created, if and how it was shared, how widely knowledge was shared (within a project team or between project teams), and whether the client was involved in the knowledge-sharing process. All our organisations engaged in continuous exchange of information, but many participants remarked that this might differ from knowledge-sharing.

Knowledge flow was regarded as knowledge-sharing only when it had the following characteristics:

◘ It was a continuous process and not just one-off question-answering.

◘ The sharing of information was combined with practice: by directly showing fellow knowledge workers how to practise a skill or by providing advice intermittently during the application of a skill.

◘ It was grounded upon a shared understanding of what the skill is. The social construction of competence through working together closely over an extended period of time was therefore important to knowledge-sharing.

We identified particular units within which the sharing of knowledge took place. Firstly, most organisations developed skills and shared problem solutions within a *project team* unit of analysis. This team structure was the main unit with whom employees identified. The importance of this was exaggerated in some firms where the project team worked for a single client, perhaps over a duration of several months or even years.

The strength of the relationships within the project team was demonstrated both through the physical layout in the firms (members of the project team would be seated in close proximity or at one laboratory bay) and in the frequency of interaction. During our site visits knowledge workers in one project team would engage in conversation about a particular problem, stand huddled over a single computer screen giving opinions about a possible solution or e-mail one another asking questions

relating to difficulties with the project. The project team often set social boundaries as well as professional boundaries as team members engaged in work conversations after hours.

In a few of our case organisations the project team boundaries appeared to be very solid – there was little interaction with other teams, and employees felt isolated and frustrated because they were not learning new skills. Having weak relationships between project teams is regarded as a barrier to success in knowledge-intensive processes. The main reason for this is that strong links between various employees in an internal knowledge network serve as a map/guidebook for 'knowing who to ask' when skills development is needed.

There are people to ask but you need to let people know who to ask.

(respondent at Ingenta)

I don't know what goes on in other project teams.

(another respondent at Ingenta)

Most of our participants believed that the ability to identify experts in an organisation, who can then be approached with technical questions, was at the heart of internal knowledge-sharing processes. This identification process can also be referred to as the building of social capital, by which relationships are developed between employees that then serve a developmental function in the organisation, thereby linking social capital to organisational competence.

Barriers that caused difficulties in building the necessary social capital, however, included the time taken up by having to identify the experts to apply to, the overall size of the organisation, and the internal focus within the project team.

'…commitment to employee development and to employee participation in decision-making were the underpinning values in this culture type.'

What is important is knowing where the expertise lies.

(respondent at MPC)

Regardless of these barriers we found that one explanatory variable influenced the knowledge-sharing processes between project teams. This variable can best be understood as the nature of the boundaries between various teams. Where boundaries were permeable, knowledge flowed freely between various teams and technical development time was reduced significantly. On the other hand, impermeable boundaries led to the hoarding of knowledge within a project team and 'a reinvention of the wheel' each time the organisation received similar project work.

The permeability of boundaries was influenced by the transcending organisational culture which forged project teams together. We found that the commitment to employee development and to employee participation in decision-making were the underpinning values in this culture type. Such values were represented by having several structures in place that overlapped with the project team structure.

For example, a working group, responsible for strategic decisions, might be established and include members from several project teams, or a mentoring system might be set up in which a mentor is involved in the development of employees from other project teams. Multi-boundary and multi-project team structures facilitate the permeability of team boundaries and encourage knowledge flow throughout the organisation.

Several technological and interpersonal networks supported these knowledge-sharing processes. In some organisations an intranet was developed on which employees would record their latest technical interest, new skills that were learned on a specific project, a fair amount of detail on projects in progress, and workloads that indicated general availability for skill development. Such software tools were successful in the facilitation of knowledge-sharing only if interpersonal knowledge networks were already in place and used frequently.

In some cases where the management of knowledge flow was solely by technological means, the intranet was simply not understood, accepted or used, thereby causing greater cynicism on the part of knowledge workers toward management-initiated knowledge-sharing projects. In this way such formal mechanisms for knowledge-sharing reflected rather than overcame these internal boundaries.

Knowledge-sharing between project teams can therefore only be successful if it is a natural way of working or embedded in the organisational routines. It has to be a practice accepted and developed by knowledge workers, rather than a policy imposed from above by a management team. Notwithstanding the importance of sharing-based work practices, all our participants believed that knowledge work could not be conducted in any other way – sharing what you know and asking others about what you don't was inherent in knowledge-intensive work.

This finding is important because it points to the need to question barriers in organisations where knowledge flow is hindered – and it highlights the deep-rooted nature of these barriers.

'Client involvement helps to build the trust between the KIF and the client...'

Knowledge-sharing between organisations

KIFs often work for a relatively small number of clients, and sometimes alongside other suppliers. Ideally, they seek stable, long-term, high-value-added contracts which take full advantage of their intellectual capital. The quality of their client and market capital – that is, their knowledge of the industry and potential clients, and the relevant knowledge-sharing processes – is vital to their success. More indirectly, their ability to acquire and keep interesting, advanced and demanding work provides an incentive for their highly mobile employees to stay with them.

KIFs often gain contracts by being invited to tender for business or to prepare a proposal for a project. However, before that happens, they have to establish a reputation in the industry for their own type of work. This might be by making formal presentations, publishing research reports, or gaining publicity through successful reference sites. Or they may simply become known through informal knowledge-sharing channels in the industry for having expertise in a certain field – for example, the ability to tackle certain types of problem and develop solutions – and attract business because of it.

Once their reputation is established, they are in a good position to develop a trusting relationship with their clients. Their employees therefore need excellent knowledge of both the industry and market trends as well as information about potential clients and their products and services.

When an invitation to bid has been received, the problem has then to be diagnosed and a proposal prepared. On occasion, however, the problem itself may be ambiguous – as one of the software engineers we interviewed put it:

Sometimes you will get a call from a client who has a very vague idea of what they want. They don't know what to expect from you, and you are not clear about how your skills can be used to solve their problem.

Knowledge-sharing in this context involves negotiation between company employees and company clients as the employees seek a relationship to reduce the ambiguity and construct specifications for the project. In the absence of this negotiation process, where the boundaries between the KIF and the client are impermeable, the ambiguity remains high and the employees are left investing longer periods of time speculatively on a project, perhaps producing several versions of a solution, all without necessarily securing repeat business from the specific client.

This emphasises the importance of client involvement in knowledge-sharing. Client involvement helps to build the trust between the KIF and the client, which is essential for recognising competence and developing professional respect (Baumard, 1999; Bontis, 1998; Leonard-Barton, 1995; Nonaka, 1994). Even if the problem is clear-cut, the preparation of a proposal will severely test the internal knowledge-sharing processes as well as the skills and knowledge of individual employees, especially when time is short. There is a need to draw together expertise from previous projects and other sources of market research and intelligence.

If the bid is successful and the contract is gained, a project team will be assembled to work either full-time dedicated to that client, or part-time alongside business for other clients. Issues of managing relations between the client, the project team and the wider KIF organisation become critical at this point. Relations with the client have to be managed, including understanding and responding to the client's needs and keeping the client up-to-date with progress. In simple situations contact is with only one part of the client organisation and good relations may be relatively easy to establish and maintain. In more complex situations, contact is with a variety of different parts of the client organisation. Indeed, the supplying KIF may effectively be providing a means of internal knowledge-sharing for the client as it pieces together the disparate parts of the client's internal structure.

It is also important to maintain relations between the client and the project team. This may be managed through a single, senior contact such as a project manager or director, or through a variety of senior and junior staff. These client relationship roles require an ability to be both client-facing and project-team-facing, to be able to translate and reconcile the requests of the client and the wishes of the members of the project team. On some occasions client requests, or demands, may place enormous strain on project teams, especially when these change at short notice.

In other instances these relations may be managed jointly by a hybrid team made up of employees of both the client and the supplying KIF. Sometimes such hybrid teams form a strong identity through which the boundaries between the different organisations virtually, but not completely, disappear. Indeed, one danger here is that a hybrid team will form such a close-knit group that it becomes isolated from their employing organisations. Where this happens, the team may effectively inhibit any advantage that might have been built up by developing their human capital through sharing knowledge internally.

KIFs also collaborate informally or formally with various other partners. Informal collaboration may be through networks of contacts linked to higher-education authorities or professional associations. These informal external knowledge networks often provide the means for updating and sustaining the customer and market capital which is vital to gaining new business. Sharing knowledge in this way through friends and colleagues who happen to work for other firms can seem quite natural – especially where there is a shared disciplinary background, such as chemistry, or a common software language. A 'collegiate' atmosphere develops, often supported by various forms of social capital, which easily permeates organisational boundaries. Such informal networks may also be supplemented by market research and other secondary data-gathering activities from written and electronic sources.

More formal collaboration between suppliers is required by some clients. Indeed, KIFs may be required to work together to produce a seamless product or service for the client. This kind of co-operation does not always come easily because the collaboration sometimes involves suppliers who are effectively competitors. However, the demands of the client will require the partners to co-ordinate their activities to break down the organisational boundaries that might act as barriers to knowledge-sharing. Issues of intellectual property rights and commercial confidentiality are likely to provide further obstacles to the required level of knowledge-sharing. This requires a high degree of trust between the partners, which usually takes a long time to develop.

In summary, we have identified knowledge-intensive situations that are critical to the success of a KIF. The management of these situations is considered a core competence and central to the innovation process. Three critical knowledge situations were identified:

◘ knowledge creation through learning-by-doing – Here the individual knowledge worker creates new knowledge through challenging work assignments and exploring alternative solutions to client problems

◘ knowledge-sharing within organisations – The key process in these situations is the sharing of know-how between project teams within one organisation – ie learning from projects

◘ knowledge sharing between organisations – These situations give both the KIF, its partners (where they exist) and the client a competitive advantage through the development of more effective solutions within a shorter timespan. Knowledge flow across organisational boundaries must be managed and encouraged.

Having identified the key knowledge-intensive situations, we now discuss people management practices in these situations that are associated with success. A KIF must manage both the *flow of knowledge* and *human resource processes* in order perform well.

Endnote

1   Redundant time corresponded to time set aside for self-managed skill development accounted for under chargeable hours but not billed to any particular client.

5 | HR practices in knowledge-intensive situations

In the previous chapter we presented three knowledge-intensive situations critical to the success of KIFs. The three situations were:

◘ learning-by-doing

◘ knowledge-sharing within an organisation

◘ knowledge-sharing between organisations.

Because these situations are central to a KIF's performance, it is important that the people management practices in the KIF address the challenges of each knowledge-intensive situation. This chapter reviews the distinctive features of the HR practices and processes in these situations, indicating how people management can influence the success of the firm. For this purpose we identify themes in sets of practices in surviving and growing KIFs, thereby linking people management and performance.

We discuss both the characteristics and the 'content' of the practices. During our interviews, many participants referred to people management practices in their organisations as a widespread range of 'approaches' that have been put in place to get the right people in, continually update skills (for which they compete) and motivate people. In our discussion we refer to the 'sets of practices' that were evident in our high-performing KIFs and that therefore deviate somewhat from the traditional descriptions of HR practices.

Closely linked to the interwoven nature of these people management practices was their embedded quality. We found that in the organisations where knowledge-intensive situations were managed successfully, people management was 'part of the way we do things'. The practices grew from within the firm and were widely adopted. It was not

merely a case of adopting 'best practice' people management practices but rather of the unfolding of appropriate practices within each particular KIF. Such embedded practices also allowed a firm to create knowledge and manage successfully within a turbulent market environment.

We focus on practices we found to be central to the successful and surviving KIFs – practices that were identified and confirmed through thematic analysis. All of them contributed to managing the knowledge-intensive situations, although some were particularly suited to specific situations. The first five we look at are thus oriented towards attracting, developing, rewarding and retaining human capital, whereas the remainder tend to be associated more with sharing knowledge within the organisation and between organisations.

◘ the importance of attracting and retaining talent within a talent war

◘ the development of human capital through work organisation and exposure to challenging projects as a tool to develop cutting-edge skills

◘ reward in the form of 'redundant' time for development

◘ the centrality of performance management in KIFs

◘ the 'intensification' of social capital (knowing who to ask, when to ask, and what to ask about when trading in a knowledge currency)

◘ managing clients and relationships with other partners in external networks.

These practices were also found to have the greatest degree of influence on intermediate

> 'In most...KIFs there was a standard procedure for recruitment, but in our interviews it was clear that the "theory-in-use" differed substantially from "formal procedures".'

performance measures such as employee motivation, commitment and loyalty. Each of these practices will now be discussed in greater depth.

Throughout this discussion we acknowledge that these HR practices are integrated to achieve certain outcomes. We are also mindful of the fact that in most of our KIFs there were multiple HR bundles of practices present to achieve a variety of strategic outcomes. Our analysis focused, however, on the most prominent practices in successful KIFs as well as on deriving a thematic representation of the qualitative data of intermediate performance measures such as employee motivation.

Attracting human capital: the talent war

The process of recruitment and selection had very distinctive characteristics in the successful KIFs. Such practices often deviated from formal policies and so were more successful if informal processes were embedded in organisational practices. Key themes that we identified from these practices were:

- networking for talent

- continuous recruitment rather than filling a vacancy only as and when one appeared

- culturally driven selection.

The successful KIFs in our sample relied on their external networks to recruit knowledge workers. In most of the KIFs there was a standard procedure for recruitment, but in our interviews it was clear that the 'theory-in-use' differed substantially from 'formal procedures'.

Recruitment was seen as a continuous process, one in which knowledge was exchanged by

developing 'talent networks' and by integrating human capital and organisational knowledge in the quest for superior intellectual capital.

Many of the organisations forged relationships with universities, competitors and professional bodies in order to have direct access to a pool of relevant talent, or knowledge workers.

A formalised way of developing networks for recruitment is the placement system – graduates and postgraduates are given the opportunity to work for the KIF for a fixed period. During this time the placement student is encouraged to develop organisation-specific skills (organisational knowledge) while other employees learn cutting-edge skills from the placement employee, through shared practice (Cook and Seely Brown, 1999).

Informal methods were also used to attract talent to the organisations. Employees were encouraged to maintain links with their former universities as well as with colleagues in previous places of work. Through these informal networks possible vacancies were discussed and employees with unique skills became known. These 'talent networks' became the eyes and ears of the recruitment process.

We know people with hot skills in the industry really through uni friends and by just meeting in the pub on Fridays with other techies.
(a respondent from MPC)

The talent networks are characterised by continuous interaction – conversation about cutting-edge skills and about who is doing what and moving where takes place continuously. The recruitment process matches this 'rhythm of conversation', and when a KIF is made aware that a certain skill is available in the labour market, the skill involved is often purchased, whether permanently or over a fixed period. It is therefore the supply of unique knowledge, and the need to integrate this knowledge into the organisation, that drives recruitment, and not a vacancy that is identified when someone leaves the organisation or when additional work is taken on by the KIF. The process of recruiting for specific talent is vastly different from recruiting to fill a vacancy.

The next theme that we identified in our data almost stands in contrast to what we have noted above. Although talent and knowledge drive recruitment, it is extremely important for these organisations that the employees they select will 'fit in with the organisation or the team'. In this sense the recruitment process is equally driven by the culture of the organisation – as the following vignette illustrates.

In relation to the tight labour market, MPC has extremely strict selection criteria. Technical ability is not considered the most important element, and it is the MPC culture that leads the recruitment process. As the senior software engineer who shares the responsibility for recruitment remarked:

I think of it as inviting someone to a party. You know sometimes you invite people who you want to come along, not necessarily those who deserve to come along.

Respondents from other organisations confirm this approach to what they are looking for in a recruit:

A sociable, not too introverted, self-confident person – the sort of person you would enjoy working with.

(a respondent from Marlborough Stirling)

Interaction with others – it is very important to fit into the company and the social life here.

(from Tocris Cookson)

Would they fit into the culture?

(from Microgen Kaisha)

They need to blend in with the team.

(another from Microgen Kaisha)

The importance of selecting knowledge workers that fit into the organisational culture is reflected in recent literature. The focus of the debate here is on the establishing of an organisational identity in the face of competing professional and client identities (Alvesson, 1995, 2000, 2001; Robertson and Swan, 1998; Starbuck, 1992; Swart *et al*, 2001). In the recruitment and retention process, identity becomes a significant object of management control and regulation to accomplish a 'subjectivity base' for the right kind of action (Alvesson, 2001: 877). Endeavouring to fit in with the organisational culture also demonstrates willingness on the part of the knowledge worker to acquire organisation-specific skills – a critical advantage in the talent war between rival KFIs.

The acquisition of organisation-specific skills acts further as a protective retention mechanism for the smaller firms that we studied. Our interviewees several times mentioned that the KIFs could be used by employees as a training ground for the larger firms, in that they might capitalise on the exposure to challenging projects at a high level and then take their enhanced skills to larger competitors. The knowledge specificity served as a safeguard in these situations and ensured that skills were less transferable between competitors. Such culturally driven recruitment can be regarded as an informal control of skill specificity which

> 'Recruits must show how they will share their innovative ideas and cutting-edge know-how within a project team.'

within a knowledge-competitive market could create competitive advantage.

The importance of fitting in with the organisational culture has the added dimension of establishing knowledge networks within the organisation. Several of the successful KIFs reported that it was relatively easy to establish whether a prospective employee had the necessary technical/professional knowledge, but the real challenge was in ascertaining whether this knowledge could be communicated in such a way that other employees could learn from this process. The communication of knowledge held was seen as a key selection criterion.

Another characteristic considered central to success at MPC, which therefore takes centre stage in the selection process, is the ability to communicate ideas together with knowledge. Recruits must show how they will share their innovative ideas and cutting-edge know-how within a project team. This forms the basis upon which the knowledge network works (as one senior employee specifically referred to it).

The establishment of knowledge networks, skill specificity and knowledge creation through recruitment was closely linked to the approach taken to development in the KIFs. Both processes were informal, embedded and employee-driven.

Another key characteristic of the recruitment process in most of our case organisations was the tendency to recruit graduates and then to focus on the development of skills within the organisation. This may have been due to the particular level of skills required, but our data suggest that this trend is linked to a wider knowledge-intensive phenomenon: the development of organisation-specific knowledge as a core competence within knowledge-intensive situations.

Developing human capital

The development of human capital was central to the knowledge-intensive situations that we identified – without the creation of knowledge (often via learning-by-doing), little value-added knowledge-sharing could take place. Most of our case organisations therefore identified the development of human capital as a key people management practice in the establishment of competitive advantage.

A key characteristic of the development of human capital in the successful KIFs was that the acquisition of a skill could not be separated from participation and workplace learning (as part of a project team). Development was therefore regarded as an informal process, driven by the demand for cutting-edge skills. The knowledge workers, and not the organisation, owned what would traditionally be known as training and development. Only one organisation in our sample had a formal training function, but even there development was driven by the employees so that the 'Academy' acted more as a resource centre where a variety of soft skills was developed. This may be attributed to the size and rapid growth of Marlborough Stirling.

Further characteristics of the successful development of human capital which we identified include:

- The unit within which development takes place may be described as a community of practice. The boundaries of such a community include various project teams and other informal networks. Membership of multiple communities is often facilitated through the use of a mentoring system.

'Each team takes responsibility for development in a unique way.'

☐ Knowledge-sharing and skill development are culturally driven by the sharing of an organisation's vision.

☐ Work design plays a key role in ensuring that critical skills are developed, and subsequently acts as a staff retention mechanism.

The unit of development: communities and project teams

The capital creation process (Tsoukas, 1996) was driven by knowledge-sharing within projects and learning across boundaries between projects. The project structure is consequently the main vehicle for the formal and informal development of resources. Within the project structure in most of the KIFs a project manager was assigned to manage the client relationship as well as the workflow within the project. However, in one of the case organisations the *most competent* person was selected to manage a project. This was often a junior member of staff who might, as a result, have a director reporting to him or her. Here everyone was given the opportunity to acquire management skills, and those who did not want to take this route in their careers had the opportunity to be project engineers (developing) and advisers (working on another project but giving advice in their area of specialisation).

Here we don't have people who do only project management – and quite honestly, with the kind of [bespoke] work we do you will never find someone who would want to do only project management work: it would be far too boring and we want to keep our skills at the cutting edge.

(respondent from MPC)

The fluidity of the project structure was a key determinant of learning and development within the organisation. Knowledge workers were rotated between projects to maintain a level of interesting work and to broaden their technical skill range. On average, employees in the more successful firms rotated between projects more frequently than their less successful counterparts. Knowledge workers in the latter group spoke of boredom with a project and an inability to acquire new skills that might in time damage their careers. On the other hand, the employees who were exposed to new projects and challenges were more committed to the organisation, were willing to share knowledge, and felt positive about their future careers.

Ingenta does not have a formal training plan. Development is employee-initiated and informal – the project team is considered the main vehicle for skill enhancement. Each team takes responsibility for development in a unique way. In some project teams development is as informal as asking for assistance on a certain task in the project. Other teams arrange training awaydays at which a facilitator is invited to address them on team-building and each team is given an opportunity to share 'new' codes that they have developed.

Team-based learning is prominent within teams, but work-based learning took place to a lesser extent between teams or across team boundaries. The difficulty of cross-team learning is increased by the multi-national nature of the organisation. Videoconferencing has been found not to be an effective medium for work-based learning.

Another central theme in the more successful KIFs was the establishing of sub-projects in response to client circumstances as well as for employee development. Sub-projects were constructed in negotiation with the clients as they moved into new markets and experienced new challenges. Such sub-projects addressed the upgrading of certain features or operation in a new market, and required knowledge of the client and market developments. Sub-project teams were often set up to teach new employees organisation-specific skills and to introduce them to key clients in the organisation. Furthermore, the sub-projects were used as an effective rotation vehicle to integrate existing skills into new product designs and to give employees the opportunity to use current knowledge in the application of new market developments.

As the projects and sub-projects intertwined and progressed, employees first struggled with challenging situations alone and then worked together to learn from one another. The main dilemma that an organisation may be faced with here is how to balance self-teaching (which is time-intensive) and group learning (which may encourage groupthink). Learning from 'the master' is highly valued within the project structure, and if 'the master' is not within the project, it is the responsibility of the project manager to point the individual employee in the right direction in order to develop the specific technical skill.

It is clear that the project structure and the work conversations undertaken within this structure served as a base to develop social capital. It was through working on several different projects with several different knowledge workers who specialise in several different areas that a knowledge network was built up in the successful KIFs. In these organisations there was a clear indication that employees knew who to ask, what to ask, and when to ask questions in order to develop both their own skills and enhance the competitive position of the organisation.

If the development of technical and organisation-specific skills were important to enhance the competitive position of the firms, however, most of the KIFs acknowledged that the professional

development of their employees was central to their retention. Development structures were therefore put in place alongside the project and sub-project teams. These structures had the purpose of stimulating the career development of the knowledge worker and exposing each employee to other areas of development within the organisation.

In most of the organisations this was achieved through a formal mentoring system. The mentoring structure had different boundaries from that of the project structure, and here employees were given the opportunity to hold conversations with their mentors specifically about their skill development. Mentors often arranged skill workshops, visiting lecturers and conferences in order to develop their protegés' skills.

The interlinked project, sub-project and mentoring structures are what give tacit knowledge in KIFs its supreme importance. The skills that must be developed are often embedded in experience, and written specifications and taught, formal courses are not able to convey these valuable tacit skills. It is in communities that work together on solving a particular problem, developing a process or synthesising a chemical that experience-based knowledge is shared and embedded skills developed. Tacit knowledge transfer is therefore practice-based, and the community experience while relying on a common language and purpose and fluid boundaries also promotes staff retention.

Nothing can beat experience – for example, picking up throw-away lines in journals, seeing products you can do something about, understanding the drugs company attitudes and knowing how to negotiate.

(a respondent from Tocris Cookson)

Culturally driven development

Integration into the way of working through experienced chemists – this is how they get used to the 'ways of the company'. That is why we recruit straight out of academia and grow the commercial experience here.

(a respondent from Tocris Cookson)

Due to the tacit nature of the skills in the KIFs, and the consequent unsuitability of formal training, most development is, as the quotation above suggests, driven by the organisational culture. The development of human capital in an organisation-specific manner ('the ways of the company') also enables the smaller organisations to retain their key knowledge workers – the more specific a skill is to the individual firm, the less transferable it becomes. This form of human capital development may have adverse effects on the career development of the respective employees.

In our exploration of the willingness of knowledge workers to engage in this type of development, we found that

◻ a clear organisational vision

◻ a sense of identification with a community in the organisation

facilitated knowledge-sharing.

The following case example illustrates these themes.

In Ingenta most participants felt that they received respect from management for their technical ability, and they also respected the quality of their colleagues' skills. As one of the directors phrased it:

You are very aware that you are working with smart, highly skilled professionals, and soon their work ethic rubs off onto you. I think this is the single most important thing that keeps people motivated – more so than which HR practices you have in place.

Participants believed that a sense of an academic community was maintained. The 'professional respect' amongst employees was strengthened further by an unshakable belief in what these skills were applied to. In other words, employees believed in the purpose for which they were using their skills.

You feel good about what you are doing. We are the backbone of research – this makes you feel important.

The belief in the purpose of the business was clearly communicated by a charismatic leader at the inception of the business, and this vision is recalled yearly, both through personal communication by the CEO and via a birthday party celebration. During these rituals the history (rags to riches) of the company is revisited and everyone is reminded of the part he or she played in the business's success.

You feel that you are part of success. You see that the vision you were told about is coming into reality.

Work design as development

We keep skills up to date by interesting and varied work, conferences and academic journals.

(respondent from Tocris Cookson)

Current literature emphasises the central role played by challenging work/projects and the subsequent skill development process in the motivation of knowledge workers. Our data confirmed this trend: we found that 'interesting work' and challenging projects were the key attraction, retention and developmental forces.

The knowledge worker's needs for interesting work therefore had a direct consequence for the business strategy. It was important to attract high-quality clients and to give employees the opportunity to engage in challenging work. The business strategy was driven by these forces – and a decision to go down the product rather than the process route could be fatal. This finding goes beyond mere resource allocation and conveys implications for business strategy, work design and workflow.

In the successful firms we studied, these processes were formalised and great care was taken to ensure that each role included exposure to various skill sets. Included in the work design was an allowance for 'redundant time' during which employees explored 'new skills' mainly through Internet sites and professional networks both internal and external to the organisation. It was clear that there was a fusion between interpersonal and technological, internal and external methods of learning and knowledge-sharing.

The fluidity of the project structure noted earlier served as a basis for innovative workflow. Here knowledge workers, through project rotation, took the initiative to contribute to different projects and learn from advisers on other project teams. The work design and the workflow, together with a shared organisational vision and identification with a community in the organisation, enabled the development of cutting-edge skills. The case example below illustrates the importance of work design on employee motivation.

A key factor in the attraction and retention of knowledge workers in MPC is the nature of the work conducted by the organisation. Employees get the opportunity to work on cutting-edge technology and to ensure that their skills remain at the forefront of this fast-changing industry. As one employee remarked:

If you ask people here what the best thing about this place is, besides the atmosphere, people will say it is the interesting work. You are always learning something new – you will never get bored.

The challenging work appears to be more critical to retention than the salary levels, for MPC do not pay better than their competitors in the local area. Employees are more focused on the quality of life that the small, innovative organisation can offer them. A senior manager felt that

You can only pay people more to keep them – but here we do not have a problem with that: the people enjoy the type of work.

Rewarding human capital

Money does not encourage performance. The most important thing is to develop an environment of autonomy, professional respect and support for decisions taken.
                    (respondent from Microgen Kaisha)

Stock options are ineffective because they are long-term and limited.
                    (from Marlborough Stirling)

The profit-sharing scheme does not work because people contribute on a daily basis and reward is only given once a year. We need to link this more clearly to the individual role.
                    (from Tocris Cookson)

'Within this context, recognition – both individual and team-based – was regarded as a more important motivator.'

The successful KIFs recognised the significance of the link between organisational and professional identity (see previous chapter) on the one hand and reward on the other. Within this context, recognition – both individual and team-based – was regarded as a more important motivator. The various forms of recognition included respect from colleagues and recognition as an expert in a certain field of expertise, as well as the recognition of exceptional performance, such as the mastering of a particularly complex task. The opportunity to develop skills other than those central to the organisation was also considered a form of recognition and reward.

More developmental forms of recognition may have been valued by the employees because of the ambiguity that is associated with monetary reward. In all our case organisations participants remarked that it was difficult to compare salary points to market surveys. This was due to the size differences between their own organisations and the larger organisations represented in the surveys. It was also felt that roles in the smaller organisations included a wide range of responsibilities and could not be compared with similar roles in other organisations. In two instances external consultants were employed to investigate comparable pay points between the KIF and its competitors. The knowledge workers met the results with great cynicism, however, commenting that cultural issues and skill specificity were not taken into account.

Our data therefore indicate a general trend in which most knowledge workers are less interested in what they get paid but more interested in what they can learn. The respect that they got from fellow knowledge workers appeared to enhance their professional identities, and these key practices enabled the sharing of knowledge both within and between organisations. Such issues are closely linked to the ways of measuring performance.

Identifying and measuring employee performance

In much professional work, the criteria for evaluating work are unreliable or entirely absent.

(Alvesson, 2001: 867)

The process of performance management at both individual and team levels is complex because knowledge-intensive outcomes tend to be highly ambiguous, yet knowledge workers have a particularly acute need for recognition. The result is that the performance management system is an especially sensitive issue in all the KIFs in our sample. Issues that intensify this include:

- the commitment to the performance management system – in particular how the outcomes within the system are determined

- the ownership of the system, including its origin

- chargeable time devoted to the system

- the links of the performance outcome to either reward or development

- the role of the performance management system in building social capital.

The knowledge workers in our sample were sensitive about their professional identity – about how fellow-workers regarded their levels of competence. According to our participants one of the most formal ways in which this identity is established is through discussing performance outcomes/achievements. There was

> 'Being able to judge performance was therefore part of an individual's own experience as a knowledge worker.'

acknowledgement that informal conversations and 'learning transactions' contributed to professional respect.

However, the record-keeping and in some cases 'public display' of performance achievements meant that the performance management system was laden with emotions. It could be argued that this is true in many other organisations, but we found that it has even greater impact in KIFs because the performance management system was often the only formalised people management system in such organisations.

The level of formality was also surprising. Even in a 30-person organisation, between six to eight performance records were kept per employee per year. The quantity of records kept and the formality of the process were seldom superficial: most employees knew exactly when performance discussions were held and what their outcomes were linked to, and could recall detailed outcomes from previous discussions. Reference was often made to their own records that were kept of these discussions.

The extent to which the performance management system was embedded in the KIFs was related to its origin. Knowledge workers themselves frequently took ownership of the development and implementation of the performance management system. There was a sense that because performance outcomes are ambiguous it was best left to the knowledge workers themselves to devise a system (generally competency- or points-based) that could differentiate between levels of performance. This emphasises the socially constructed nature of these performance outcomes.

How competent the individual is as a knowledge worker, how much the individual knows, and the value the individual adds on behalf of the clients are determined through a negotiation process. It was the working together in project teams, learning from 'the master', constantly judging one's own and others' competence, that established the performance negotiation process. Being able to judge performance was therefore part of an individual's own experience as a knowledge worker. Tacit knowledge and tacit skill were the backbone of performance management.

The nebulous quality of the performance measured/judged, together with a rather nebulous process of judging performance, and the sensitivity surrounding the outcome of this process, meant that knowledge workers tended to devote a great deal of their time to this system. In the successful KIFs the process went through several iterations without any sign of demotivation. The strong sense of ownership together with involvement in the design of the process established this sense of commitment.

In Microgen Kaisha, senior and principal members of staff dedicated some of their chargeable time to the running of the performance management system. Employees are assigned reviewers that 'fit' their employment profile. The consultancy manager manages the process of assigning reviewers. Performance reviewers would follow their appraisees on client visits. Such observations would then be followed by developmental discussions and the completion of a detailed project assessment form. Further performance data are gathered from project managers, from peers on the same project and from the client. Before each performance discussion the employee would be given an opportunity for self-assessment. Detailed comparisons of the 360-degree review are then recorded for future developmental and reward purposes.

When we questioned the performance reviewers in the above case about the sacrifice of their chargeable time, the perception was that they were not reducing their fee-earning potential but that they were strengthening the organisation by developing employees and by building networks for performance feedback.

This theme was confirmed in several of our other successful organisations: performance management was regarded as a tool to build social capital. Latham and Wexley (1981) also found that performance appraisals could be used to outline and reinforce behavioural norms and build social capital.

Performance reviews were the key system that enabled knowledge workers to bridge several boundaries:

◻ An employee outside the core project team conducted performance reviews.

◻ Clients were often involved in performance evaluation.

◻ Teams of performance reviewers would often meet to discuss the process of evaluation as well as the subsequent developmental options, thereby establishing another community of practice.

◻ The outcome of a performance discussion would frequently be linked to further development, which in these KIFs translated into workplace learning. This reinforced the organisation-specific skill acquisition and accounted for the culturally driven nature of development.

◻ During performance discussions, knowledge workers were often made aware of 'experts' whom they could approach when working on a relevant project. This strengthened the knowledge network and answered the all-important question of 'knowing who to ask'.

Social capital

Knowledge-sharing within and between organisations was identified as a knowledge-intensive situation that may be considered critical to a KIF's success. However, the sharing of knowledge can take place only within well-established networks where employees have developed a shared understanding of processes in the organisation. These informal networks that enhance social and knowledge exchange can be described as social capital.

Organisational social capital has been loosely defined as a firm asset that is embedded in the relationships of employees and managers within the firm (Nahapiet and Goshal, 1998). Social capital is also often portrayed as internal and external firm networks. A traditional network perspective incorporates the set of linkages between an actor or set of actors and the various contacts with which the actor interacts (Burt, 1982). These networks, and especially the links between actors/sets of actors, are of particular importance in KIFs. In view of the fact that the central form of capital is intangible (knowledge) and that the success of the firm depends on knowledge creation, the reliance on linking various 'nodes of knowledge' is regarded as a core competence in knowledge-intensive situations.

The linking of nodes and the strength of these links are dependent upon several factors.

'Where project team boundaries were fluid, networks were spidered across the organisation, thereby building social capital.'

Firstly, the frequency of interaction will influence the strength of nodal linkages. We found that a high degree of interaction between knowledge workers positively influenced the strength of employee relationships. This is where the design of project teams had a major role to play. Where project team boundaries were fluid, networks were spidered across the organisation, thereby building social capital. However, in organisations where project teams were too large and felt isolated, networks were limited, and when vital knowledge questions required an answer, answers were provided only for the immediate project team, thereby limiting knowledge creation.

Secondly, knowledge networks were reinforced by participative cultures in our successful organisations. Employees 'owned' and took responsibility for many of the people management processes. Strategic decisions were discussed at operational level, and in the absence of traditional departments a few of the growing KIFs relied upon working groups to design and implement operating systems. In this sense the successful organisations relied upon knowledge networks to develop skills and upon operational networks to make and implement key decisions. Social capital was at the heart of most business processes.

A third influence on the development of social capital was the reinforcement of behavioural norms. Here we identified two key management practices that directly influenced behaviour. The first was the establishment of organisational identity – an image that knowledge workers could identify with and could take upon themselves to become part of the community of knowledge workers in the KIF. Alvesson (2001) describes corporate identity as constructions of what the company stands for and of the respects in which it is more or less unique.

Recent literature also refers to the dedication of management to the construction of corporate identities. This is because the knowledge-intensive environment is ambiguous – staff turnover tends to be high because professional employees want to gain maximum exposure to exciting projects, and it is important for knowledge workers to have a sense of professional group identity (other than by belonging to a professional body). A strong organisational identity, which is often coupled with culturally driven people management practices is an important criterion for building social capital.

The second set of practices used to enforce behavioural norms in order to strengthen relationship links is the performance management system. Here competent behaviour is identified, evaluated and rewarded, thereby reinforcing the organisation-specific practice of a technical skill. Employees are rewarded for the enactment of behavioural norms and for 'learning from the master'. In this context the sharing of tacit skill and the continuous strengthening of these skills are used to build social capital. As Wenger (2000) suggests, it is through legitimate participation that 'we know what we know' and 'who to ask if we don't know'. This is the essence of KIFs and why social capital is so central to their survival and success.

The performance management system can also reinforce behavioural norms which effectively form obstacles to sharing knowledge. Employees may be discouraged from sharing their knowledge if individual performance is rewarded irrespective of the means the individuals have used to achieve their results. Rewarding behaviour which deliberately avoids knowledge-sharing is a particular disincentive to others. Some employees are unwilling to share their knowledge if they believe it will be 'stolen' and used by others for

'...the skills of preparing – and especially, presenting – a proposal to a client are likely to be more difficult to identify and locate.'

their own gain without suitable acknowledgement.

A case example of building social capital through involvement involves MPC.

A particular HR process in MPC that is considered critical to the retention of employees is that of participation and involvement. This process is driven by the organisational culture, and all employees are involved in major company decisions. The main formal vehicle used for its implementation is the committee, but many informal processes are also used to generate involvement. For example, during the period of growth that was then being experienced, the MD asked all employees to describe what their vision for the company was, and to identify the areas that they would like to develop their own skills into. In addition, employees feel that they can make suggestions regarding company decisions to the directors at any time on an informal basis. Their views are taken seriously. Senior employees have commented that they cannot think of one instance when suggestions have not been 'taken up into the company'. As one participant put it:

You feel you are important and you are listened to.

Developing client and market capital

Social capital is also important for developing the client and market capital, which is vital for acquiring, managing and growing contracts with clients. Client and market capital includes not just knowledge about the market conditions, technology and possible clients, but also the skills necessary for managing the relationships and networks that exist. These forms of capital help to establish reputation in the field, which is linked to being asked to tender for work and being able to attract sought-after employees.

External knowledge networks provide an excellent source of information about developments in the market, including changes in technology and the needs of potential clients. More formal means of keeping up to date include research publications and market intelligence. Identifying potential and existing employees who are good at this is relatively straightforward because many of these skills will have been learned during their professional training. However, the skills of preparing – and especially, presenting – a proposal to a client are likely to be more difficult to identify and locate. Many KIFs' employees are much more comfortable in the laboratory than in the boardroom. Indeed, some avoid contact with clients if at all possible. This places a premium on the people management practices associated with developing the skills of those who present any bid and the composition of any team that prepares the bid.

These people management practices become critical once a contract has been awarded, especially those concerned with managing potentially conflicting pressures from the client and the team assigned to that project. Some KIFs try to develop their own project managers and directors through a mix of formal and informal development and knowledge-sharing processes. Others realise they cannot develop these skills quickly enough, and try to recruit from the external labour market. One obvious source that is often used is the clients themselves, and in some knowledge-intensive sectors it is quite common for employees to move from 'client-side' to a supplying organisation and back again.

People management practices may be affected not only indirectly in this way by clients but also more

> 'People management practices are likely to be central to developing social capital, which itself allows customer and market capital to be generated.'

directly. Clients may, for example, seek to influence who works on their project and how that work is actually carried out. More formally, they may contribute to the appraisal of individual employees and to the overall evaluation of the success of the project. Consequently, employees may develop skills, in response to client requests, which are difficult to integrate and internalise in their own organisation.

Clients here are strengthening the internal boundaries between project teams in the KIF, especially if they insist that 'their' project team maintains a high level of client confidentiality. This client/project identification can undermine a strong identification with the KIF organisation which increases co-operation among its members and directs additional effort towards tasks contributing to co-workers and the organisation (Orlikowski, 2002: 258).

Furthermore, when the organisational boundaries are highly permeable, the knowledge workers tend to identify more strongly with the client than with the KIF. This creates an opportunity for a few key knowledge workers to join the client organisation or to leave the KIF and start their own organisation. If a key person leaves, the company may lose clients, because they are sometimes more interested in a particular person than in the entire company (Alvesson, 2000).

Such relationship management skills may be tested even further if the KIF is asked to collaborate formally with other suppliers. Social-capital-forming skills are again likely to be important, encouraging a common interest to be established. Employees must appreciate the need for and the importance of sharing knowledge between partners. There is a need to form an information democracy by means of open meetings, job

rotation and collegiate decision-making (Boxall and Purcell, 2003: 85; Nonaka and Takeuchi, 1995). This might involve establishing a common language which, for example, precludes references to employing organisations. However, some employees will find it especially difficult to learn how to co-operate with organisations that in the past have been and in the future may be competitors.

People management practices are also important when a hybrid team is formed that is made up of members of the client company and various suppliers. There is a clear need for people in these teams to be able to identify strongly with the interests of the project team as well as with their employing organisation on both the supplier and client sides.

In effect, we can see here the consequences of merging internal and external knowledge networks. Practices associated with team formation and team-building are likely to be particularly important. In addition, members of the teams will need experience in acting in a representative role and in the skills of negotiating with their respective organisations when key decisions – for example, on resources – have to be taken.

People management practices are likely to be central to developing social capital, which itself allows customer and market capital to be generated. In particular, their role in balancing team, organisational, professional and client identities are likely to be of critical importance.

In summary, we have presented the people management practices that were found in our successful KIFs. Here we make a clear link between knowledge-intensive situations and the people management practices that lead to positive HR outcomes in those situations. The practices we identified were:

◘ the attraction of human capital – Key themes that were identified here included networking for talent, continuous recruitment and culturally driven selection.

◘ the development of human capital that is self-directed and takes place mainly within the project team – In order to enhance the organisation-specific knowledge in the KIF, development is also culturally driven and facilitated through the design of workflow within and across teams.

◘ the process of rewarding knowledge workers – Our data suggested that 'redundant time' for development was seen as important, yet comparable pay levels did have an influence.

◘ identifying and measuring employee performance – Knowledge workers were extremely sensitive about the validity of the process through which their outputs were measured. Performance measurement also enabled employees to span several organisational boundaries and therefore facilitated the development of social capital.

◘ the development of social capital – ie the strength of the relationships within networks in the organisation – Factors which influence the building of social capital were the frequency of interaction, participative cultures, and the enforcement of behavioural norms through the establishment of an organisational identity and performance management.

◘ the identification and development of skills needed to acquire client and market capital, and those needed to manage the interests of the client, the client team, the wider employing organisation and any other partners involved in a knowledge network.

We found that in successful KIFs these HR practices were embedded in organisational routines and became part of the way in which people managed. Such evolutionary qualities rest within the notion that both strategy and policies are most successful when utilised in daily practices.

The next chapter draws together the people management practices that pertain specifically to knowledge-intensive situations, and asks the question: what are the underlying issues which the people management practices ought to address? We present three key themes that we identified in our data, and illustrate how these themes link people management to performance.

6 | Implications for people management and performance

In this chapter we draw on the key themes discussed so far and reflect on the implications for people management. In earlier chapters we first identified knowledge-intensive situations, highlighting the uniqueness of intellectual capital as the key resource in successful KIFs. We noted the importance of individual knowledge creation and reflected on how knowledge is then shared within and between organisations. The contribution of people management practices to the successful management of these organisations was subsequently considered. Our focus was on the people management practices that influence intermediate performance outcomes such as employee motivation. The characteristics of these practices were presented together with a brief summary of what 'worked' in knowledge-intensive situations.

In this chapter we aim to weave the previous discussions together within the wider framework of knowledge management, and to consider the link with performance more explicitly. With greater precision, we distinguish between our more and less successful firms using various key measures of performance. We then seek to identify the key people management issues that must be managed well if the firm is to be successful.

We believe there are three tensions which link the way people are managed and the performance of the firm. These tensions are between:

◘ managing knowledge within the organisation and managing the needs of knowledge workers

◘ balancing three key identities – organisational, professional and client

◘ striking a balance between the need for formal explicit procedures for managing people and the need for them to be informal and embedded in the routines of the organisation.

Before we look at this in more detail we should consider some of the problems with measuring success in these organisations.

Measuring performance

Early in this report we noted the volatile conditions amidst which our software firms especially were operating during this period. In such an environment simply surviving is an achievement. However, we must be more precise in our measurement of success if we are to discriminate between our firms. In short, how do we know Firm A is more successful than Firm B? We propose that success can be judged by measures of both performance or knowledge outputs and the knowledge inputs and processes.

If we consider output measures first, we define successful KIFs as the organisations with low staff turnover, growth in the number of full-time permanent employees, and an increase in percentage turnover growth during the period of research. Using these measures, all our firms were successful on different measures: all six KIFs experienced relatively low levels of staff turnover (MPC and Tocris Cookson were the lowest), all the firms had high levels of turnover growth (Ingenta and Marlborough Stirling were the highest), however, both Ingenta and Epinet had to reduce their number of full-time permanent employees. Given the complexity of the output measures we believe it is also important to pay attention to input measures.

Input measures include the extent to which knowledge is shared within the organisation and

> '...we define successful KIFs as the organisations with low staff turnover, growth in the number of full-time permanent employees, and an increase in percentage turnover growth...'

with clients. We determined the input measures through our qualitative analysis of interviews across the KIFs. The firms that are most successful in these terms are MPC and Tocris Cookson, while the firms where knowledge flows less freely across boundaries include Marlborough Stirling, Microgen-Kaisha, Epinet and Ingenta.

Having established the relative success of our cases, our task now is to explain this pattern of results – in short, what is it that makes the difference? We argue that the way each of our firms manages the tensions we have identified makes a significant contribution to their success.

Managing knowledge workers and managing knowledge

According to the knowledge-based view of the firm presented earlier, knowledge is embedded in organisational practices and routines and is therefore spread throughout the organisation. It is not contained in one individual. However, if the firm is to make the most of its intellectual capital, a participative culture must be created in which employees share what they have learned and are prepared to develop organisation-specific skills. A strong identification with the organisation is imperative to the development of an organisational knowledge-base. We examine this issue from the point of view of individual knowledge workers and the need to share knowledge within the organisation. In particular, we identify a potential tension between the needs of knowledge workers and the need for the integration of knowledge.

On the one hand employees in KIFs are looking to develop their own skills and to get involved in interesting and challenging work that tests their abilities fully. They want to develop their careers

either by internal promotion or, if necessary, by leaving the organisation. Some knowledge workers tend to be competitive and ambitious and want to remain one step ahead of the external labour pool in terms of skill development. The natural tendency is to move frequently between organisations and to gain exposure to 'the big names'. This then enables knowledge workers to work more independently as consultants to other organisations with knowledge-intensive work practices.

For example, in one of our case studies we found that employees did not want to sacrifice chargeable time on organisation-wide activities, so communication meetings were not attended, teamwork was not valued, and there was no induction training. These knowledge workers were, however, committed to the performance management process and took great care in ensuring that frequent career discussions took place.

People management practices that are more conducive to individual development and career progression include:

◘ standardised performance appraisal in order to promote from within

◘ formalised training courses that enable employees to transfer skills to another employer, thereby increasing their employability

◘ individually based reward and recognition

◘ time devoted to development external to the organisation through professional bodies

◘ standardisation of work practices, often driven by a move toward product-based design rather than bespoke services.

'...when the people management practices do not facilitate the integration of knowledge, the success of the business may be reduced.'

As we know, however, there is a strong need to share knowledge between individuals and the project teams within which they work if the maximum is to be gained from the firm's intellectual capital. There must be links between the potentially isolated pools of knowledge that are dispersed throughout the organisation. People management practices can encourage integration of employees and teams connecting various knowledge nodes within the organisation.

Practices that interweave disparate pockets of knowledge in the KIF may include:

□ participation and involvement in decision-making

□ induction training

□ mentoring

□ performance appraisal

□ team-based rewards

□ work-based learning

□ frequent social activities

□ cross-disciplinary project teams.

The two bundles of practices that facilitate the management of knowledge workers on the one hand and the management of knowledge on the other can pull in opposite directions. We found that when the people management practices do not facilitate the integration of knowledge, the success of the business may be reduced. A comple-mentary synergy between the practices for managing knowledge workers and for managing knowledge can contribute towards the success of KIFs.

Figure 3 | The tension between the management of knowledge and knowledge workers

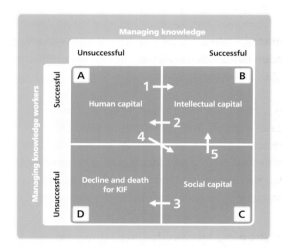

Figure 3 illustrates that the capacity to manage knowledge-based intellect in KIFs is regarded as a critical competence (Quinn, 1992) measurable against two continua. The vertical axis represents the degree of success achieved in managing knowledge workers. Firms in quadrant A, for example, have successful measures in place for attracting, developing, rewarding and retaining human capital, whereas in quadrant D employees are not well suited to the work involved and there may be high labour turnover. The horizontal axis classifies organisations on the basis of how good they are at managing and sharing knowledge internally. So, for example, firms in quadrant B are able to successfully convert their human capital into intellectual capital through the use of social capital. Firms in quadrant C, however, have good forms of social capital but do not have sufficient human capital from which to draw. Those in quadrant D in these terms have incomplete or inappropriate forms of social capital. Indeed, firms in this quadrant are likely to find it difficult to survive because they are poor in terms of both their human and social capital, and they are likely to decline and be left wondering what all the fuss is about (Bontis, 1998).

The discussion that follows addresses the people management implications of moving between these quadrants.

First, the move from quadrant A – from human capital – to intellectual capital (arrow 1) involves recruiting employees that fit into the organisational culture and would want to identify with and contribute to the organisation, as for example in Tocris Cookson. Human capital is increased through training and development. Although new employees are expected to have a high level of competence in the required skills, knowledge workers expect that they will be able to add to their skill portfolio through development within the organisation. This form of skill development is often accompanied by an expectation of transferability – consequently, skill development must be standardised in the particular industry. Such standardised development may cause the employee to leave the organisation, merely using it as a training ground.

High-performance developmental practices have to ensure that training is organisation-specific. Successful KIFs use the intellectual capital in the organisation (arrow 2 from quadrant B to quadrant A) as a developmental tool through work-based learning and self-managed development. For example, using the project team structure as the main vehicle for skill development – as at MPC – ensures that the building of human capital is integrated into the organisational routines.

Project-based development is strongly linked to the establishment of social capital (quadrant C) – it is through the face-to-face interaction in the project

that relationships form. The links between various knowledge nodes (individuals in the network) help transform and develop intellectual capital (arrow 5). A strong project-based focus may, however, leave little room for individual development and career advancement. For example, a software engineer working on a three-year client project may be requested to remain on the project due to client relationships and the specific technical knowledge held. The containment of the knowledge worker's career within the boundaries of the project (arrow 3) may have adverse effects on the employee's long-term career.

People management practices that facilitate exposure to a variety of client projects via job-rotation will enhance the intellectual capital directly (arrow 1) and more indirectly via social capital (arrow 4, followed by arrow 5). These practices can address the need for career progression of the knowledge worker and effectively control the internalisation of skill development. Within the context of social capital development it is therefore important that knowledge workers identify with the project and the organisation as a whole. The following quotation from a case demonstrates how a project focus at the expense of an organisational focus can act as a barrier to social capital.

Team spirit within the team is good – we often meet and discuss things and we are motivated within our team. But all the problems that we have experienced have been down to isolation. This slows things down, and it becomes difficult to function within the organisation.

(respondent from Ingenta)

People management practices can also fragment the organisation-wide social capital if employee participation is focused mainly at project level. This

'It is not only the project team that develops social networks: other participative structures ensure that an even richer network is developed.'

tends to lead to a feeling of control and influence at team level, which causes further fragmentation. Employees feel isolation from company-wide decisions and the team structure therefore creates a sense of identity and belonging. One research participant remarked that:

As the company grows, you have little groups that do things together. This way you get the feeling of still being a small company, but you may not know everything that the other groups are doing.

Social capital can also be built by bridging multiple boundaries in the organisation. It is not only the project team that develops social networks: other participative structures ensure that an even richer network is developed. In our successful cases, people management practices facilitated high levels of involvement in decision-making through the establishment of several working groups and committees. These sub-structures ensured that knowledge workers identified with the organisation and took responsibility for the organisation's success.

We have argued that the ability to manage the potential tension between the distribution and integration of knowledge makes a significant contribution to organisational success. One way of managing this tension is by paying attention to the differing pulls on employee loyalty – or, as we term it, types of employee identity.

Managing identities to enhance knowledge flow

In this section we describe how managing identities can help to resolve the counteracting pulls between the needs of the employees and the need to share knowledge. There are various forms of identity in the discussion that follows – team,

organisational, professional, and client. Here we highlight how each form of identity was established and consider the management processes involved in maintaining these identities. We argue that the ability to manage these identities helps us to explain the performance of our case studies.

People management practices and processes can have a direct impact on the various identities that are formed. Alvesson and Willmott (2002) argue that:

Identity regulation encompasses the more or less intentional effects of social practices upon the process of identity construction … Notably, induction, training and promotion procedures are developed in ways that have implications for the shaping and direction of identity.

A shared identity, whether it is organisational, professional or client-focused, is established by engaging in common practice (often through training and socialisation), by approaching knowledge-intensive work in a similar manner (applying skills in an organisation-/client-specific way) and by believing in a common purpose. Knowledge workers in our cases identified with their team, organisation, client and profession to varying degrees.

The management of an identity was therefore not a mutually exclusive process. The direction of identification, however, influenced the way knowledge flowed within the organisation and between the organisation and external parties. A strong identification with the organisation and colleagues meant that knowledge was shared frequently within and between project teams. Whereas a strong identification with a client combined with a weak organisational identity translated into knowledge-sharing and control by the client with limited internal shared practice and contribution to organisational solutions and routines.

In those KIFs where employees identified strongly with the organisation, most management practices were culturally driven. For example, people were recruited on the basis that they would fit in with the team or the organisation, critical strategic decisions were delayed if it was common practice to ask for input from working groups/committees, and employees often referred to certain processes as 'the way we do things here'. The organisational routines were therefore highly visible, and formal systems were in place to introduce new employees to these routines. In some cases only university students were employed, and then their practice/ skill implementation was shaped and moulded by the organisation.

Employee development was also organisation-specific and there was little evidence of formal or external training courses within the KIFs. The notion of team-based development and learning from one another in Tocris, for example, enabled new employees to become familiar with organisational routines. Through this process of socialisation, knowledge workers 'knew' the organisation and how it works.

In most of our case organisations the performance management process 'evolved' from within the KIF and can be seen as a symbol of a culturally driven process. Performance standards were organisation-specific and negotiated between knowledge workers. We found vast differences across the KIFs for individual roles, such as that of a software engineer. These different ways of expressing and appraising competencies demonstrated how organisation-specific they were. In other words,

the performance appraisal process helped employees identify with 'the way of doing things' in their particular organisation.

However, in the few cases – such as Ingenta – where an external consultant was used to develop a performance management system, employees did not demonstrate any acceptance of the system. Firstly, they believed they could not trust the system and its outcomes, such as reward, promotion and development. Secondly, various performance measures were developed in project teams, thereby creating identification with the team rather than with the organisation as a whole. Team identification then posed a threat to integration and knowledge-sharing across the organisation. It also resulted in employees' feeling less loyal to the organisation, which made it difficult to retain key members of staff.

Building social networks within the organisation strengthened the organisational identification further. It was through daily face-to-face interaction with a project team and other teams, such as committees, that a sense of belonging was created. These networks served as maps that were used to navigate around knowledge-intensive work – they served as a rough guide to the identification of and conversation with experts.

There is a strong knowledge base and everyone is keen to help out throughout the project.
(respondent from MPC)

I am interested in what the rest of the team is doing. We discuss ideas and provide support.
(from Tocris Cookson)

These social networks played another important role in establishing an organisational identity. It was through interaction in the network that the

'...in most of the case organisations committees were set up to arrange events, ranging from weekly gatherings for staff members only to monthly or biannual events that included family members.'

'story' about how the KIF started as well as its success and failures were shared. For example, in Tocris employees would hear from other chemists at their bay in the laboratory that it is an honour to work in the new building. Stories about how the owners worked at a single bench in a university, how funds were raised for the new building, and about the expansion in the USA would be told as well. Chemists remarked that 'this made you believe in what the organisation stood for' and 'you felt part of its success'.

A further prominent feature of KIFs that established a strong organisational identity was the degree of social events that were arranged within the organisation. We found that in most of the case organisations committees were set up to arrange events, ranging from weekly gatherings for staff members only to monthly or biannual events that included family members. Here the identification crossed organisational boundaries to include non-work hours as well as non-employees. Identifying with the organisation meant that it is something that a knowledge worker does all the time.

In the context of a strong organisational identification, professional networks were often encouraged. Here chemists or software engineers that specialise in certain areas would meet often, arrange workshops and distribute relevant and up-to-date reading material. The building of professional networks within and across organisations established a professional identity. However, the KIFs never considered identification with a profession as a hindrance to an organisational identity or to knowledge-sharing. Often the boundaries of professional networks spanned project team boundaries and encouraged knowledge flow throughout the KIFs. The strong identification with employees in other teams, the

practice that was shared, and the developmental focus contributed to the motivation for knowledge-sharing.

Identification with the organisation and the profession would have been of little value if the technical (professional) and organisation-specific skills could not be applied to projects with clients. Client identity therefore plays an important role in knowledge-intensive processes, and it is established through exposure to the client such as by working on the client site and in the extent to which the client wants to control work practices.

Clients' opinions are often included in performance appraisals, and it is therefore imperative that KIF employees build strong relationships with the clients to ensure that demands are met and that trust is developed between employee and client. During the process of relationship-building a knowledge worker may spend time on the client site, sit in on client training and familiarise himself/herself with the client's operational system. A certain degree of client socialisation therefore takes place, which develops identification with the client and the client-specific forms of knowledge.

There are potential dangers of too high a level of client identification. Employees may give the client's interests priority when making decisions and sharing information, perhaps to the detriment of their own employers. Too little concern for clients' interests can also be damaging, continuously placing the organisation's concerns – for example, to make sufficient margin of profit – ahead of those of the client. It is something that can leave the client disgruntled and looking to take its business elsewhere.

The effect is to place emphasis on the people management practices that can help to develop

'All employees were fully aware of the content of HR policies because of the high levels of involvement in their formulation.'

client relationship skills. Similar skills are needed when collaborating with partners in any networks that are formed. This may go against the natural inclination to compete with other firms in the industry. In some fields there is a strong association with a particular profession, along with the notion that there is a wider community of knowledge outside the organisation to which all members can contribute. The members of this community may share a similar training and disciplinary background and language which help the process of sharing knowledge.

The task is to balance the conflicting pulls of team, organisational, client and professional identities. The more successful companies are those that have designed people management practices which ensure that these identities are not mutually exclusive. Such companies have been able to resolve the final conflict we have highlighted between the need for formal policies and the need for processes that are embedded into organisational routines.

The embedded nature of HR practices

The high-performing KIFs did not rely solely on formal HR policies implanted from outside or a senior level, but were able to generate these polices from day-to-day informal practice and then to embed these policies into the organisational processes. They used highly participative processes often involving a bottom-up path of formulation, to develop policies which were respected and strictly adhered to. All employees were fully aware of the content of HR policies because of the high levels of involvement in their formulation. The policies contributed to highly formalised HR processes, which is a clear indication that HR processes were not merely left to evolve, and that

careful attention was paid to capture 'processes which work' in a more formal manner.

This raises a further key issue about the HR policies – they originate from practice and therefore reflect core organisational routines. Policies are also not bought in from external consultants or made to fit popular practice. As one senior interviewee remarked:

We need to do what works for us. One mentor may try something, and if it works it will be shared at our mentor meeting, and then – if we all agree and the directors approve it – it will be used by everyone, and we will document [the procedure] on the intranet. This is how our performance appraisal system came about anyway.
(respondent from MPC)

The embedded and almost natural quality of these practices indicated that people management evolved from the links between social and human capital – it was by skilled employees and through relationships in knowledge networks that HR practices originated. As another research participant said:

It is just part of the way we do things.

Some of the less successful companies did not pursue this inductive approach to the development of HR policies. Instead, they adopted a more top-down approach, or simply did not have any formal policies in key areas. In one case, employees rejected practices by which people management originated from a consultant brought in to solve a specific HR issue. In this instance, detailed HR policies left most line managers and employees confused and mistrusting the HR system.

I had to do a lot of reading. It [the policy] was difficult to understand, and getting hold of someone to explain how it works in practice is not easy.

(respondent from Ingenta)

In other cases there were inconsistencies in the interpretation of policies because of a lack of shared ownership or understanding. For example, one manager remarked that the policy to recruit internally hampered successful attraction if others were not aware of the policy. Policies also appeared to jar with practice – as one participant put it:

You are told that you cannot automatically give increases – but when you look closely at it, then you see that everyone gives inflationary increases.

It became accepted that 'Policies are not practised.'

In other cases formal policies were absent and people management practice emerged on an *ad hoc* basis, usually representing the low priority given to these issues. Terms such as 'haphazard', 'trial and error' and 'We make it up as we go along' were central to our analysis. This often led to a team-based focus to people management by which each team would implement different sets of practices to manage knowledge workers. The fragmentation of people management practices eventually not only led to inconsistency and perceived unfairness, but also weakened valuable intellectual capital and had an adverse effect on the competitive advantage of the KIF.

Our more successful companies allowed HR policies to emerge from practice, rather than just assuming that policy would control practice. Their ways of managing people became embedded into the organisational routines and accepted as the way things were done because they were effectively a codified form of emerging practices and routines. The less successful companies either relied on formal policies or sought to manage without any policies.

Our cases enjoy varying success when measured in terms of their performance outcomes and their knowledge inputs and processes. We have sought to explain their varying performance in terms of their ability to manage three key tensions. The first is between the interests of individual knowledge workers in developing their skills through engaging in stimulating work and the need to share knowledge throughout the organisation. One way of resolving this is by paying attention to the differing identities which employees may hold – in particular the team, organisational, professional and client identities. The firms that were particularly successful in managing these identities were those that were able to achieve a situation where their formal policies were respected and reflected and to influence practice because they had become embedded in organisational routines.

Following our consideration of the implications of our analysis of the people management in knowledge-intensive firms, in the final chapter we draw some conclusions about the links between people and performance more generally.

7 | Conclusions

This study grew out of a wider research project looking at the links between people management practices and organisational performance. In particular, we wanted to understand how people management practices might contribute to creating competitive advantage in organisations which relied upon intellectual capital as their trading assets and which operated in unstable and unpredictable markets. In this section we consider some of the broader lessons that can be drawn from this study in respect of the links between people management and performance in KIFs. Before doing this, it is useful to recall the key sections of this report.

- ◘ We began by establishing the distinctive characteristics of knowledge-intensive firms and drew attention to the knowledge of skills of the employees involved, the type of work they were engaged in, and the nature of the industry in which these firms existed.

- ◘ Following this, a series of knowledge-intensive situations were identified that are essential to the success of these organisations.

- ◘ We then examined the people management practices that contributed to the successful management of such situations and so contributed to improving firm performance.

- ◘ Finally, following an analysis of the performance of our cases, we sought to explain the variations we observed by focusing on our firms' ability to manage three key tensions which go to the heart of KIFs. In effect we were seeking to establish the core people management competences of these firms (Hamel and Prahalad, 1994).

We are now going to look at the distinctive characteristics and knowledge-intensive situations in turn to consider the contribution made by people management practices more systematically.

The first important characteristic of KIFs is that a high proportion of the employees are knowledge workers, compared, for example, with the number of support staff who are not knowledge workers. This focuses attention on the needs of these knowledge workers. They will want to work on interesting projects which make good use of their high-level knowledge and skills, involving the latest technology where possible. Consequently, importance is attached to the creation and development of knowledge at an individual level, which was referred to as 'learning-by-doing'.

The emphasis here on the characteristics of human capital highlights the role of people management practices for recruiting, developing, rewarding and retaining these employees. One aim is to bring people into the organisation who will fit in well and to provide them with opportunities to develop their skills and knowledge. This requires attention not only to skill and knowledge development through interesting work but also to the systems for rewarding employees financially.

Another aim then is to develop employee skills and knowledge that have value in the marketplace and yet will encourage employees to stay with the organisation. Failure to do this might mean that knowledge workers do not develop their potential or that their effort declines because they are bored (Boxall and Purcell, 2003: 83). Feelings of unfair reward might lead these employees to take on private work or, if they are senior, to award themselves excessive share options (Boxall and Purcell, 2003: 86). More seriously, some employees may leave – which can have either or both of two important consequences. As Boxall and Purcell

> **'KIFs are particularly vulnerable to labour turnover because although it may be possible to replace the explicit knowledge held by a person, it is much more difficult to replace his or her tacit knowledge.'**

(2003: 83) note, KIFs are particularly vulnerable to labour turnover because although it may be possible to replace the explicit knowledge held by a person, it is much more difficult to replace his or her tacit knowledge. In addition, senior members of staff may enjoy good relationships with client representatives and they may then have the power to take the client's contract with them if they leave the firm.

The second aspect of KIFs to which we drew attention was the type of work involved. If the skills of knowledge workers are applied to routine or standardised tasks, the work may be less intense compared with work in organisations that provide mostly bespoke solutions. Employees learn cutting-edge skills through novel, complex project work and by solving problems in project teams.

This emphasis on project-based work is exaggerated when a project is dedicated to a single client, perhaps over several months or years. The danger here is that the knowledge that has been developed may become distributed or dispersed throughout the organisation and held in isolated pockets. This client and project focus then makes it especially difficult to share and integrate that knowledge between the dedicated project teams. Indeed, each team may be measured on its ability to achieve its own performance targets, thereby weakening any inclination to transfer knowledge elsewhere. At its most extreme, team members, or even individual employees, may ask: 'Why should I share my secrets of success?' This can be made even worse when clients request that knowledge is not shared between project teams on the grounds that the information and skills held are confidential.

People management practices and processes can play a key role in developing social capital which encourages knowledge to be shared (Nahapiet and Ghoshal, 1998). These practices can stimulate the establishment of informal networks which help to overcome the barriers to the integration of knowledge. Employees are encouraged to exchange information through a variety of formal and informal mechanisms which link across the individual project teams. In addition, the emphasis is on creating the contexts to share tacit knowledge that is difficult to codify and exchange using IT-based systems. This might involve paying close attention to selection criteria so that those likely to share knowledge are recruited. More broadly, this involves creating an organisational culture in which openness and sharing are taken for granted. It is an environment that might be sustained by training and development programmes or by more informal methods of socialisation involving social meetings inside and outside work, perhaps also involving employees' families to create a broader attachment and loyalty to the company.

The final important aspect of KIFs is the characteristics of the industry within which they work. Many of these firms form business-to-business relationships with a relatively small number of clients, some of whom may provide a substantial percentage of the total business. In order to gain this business KIFs must acquire a good reputation for being able to demonstrate the possession of up-to-date knowledge and skills, especially if they want to attract the desirable high-value business. In addition, some KIFs work in collaboration with a number of other suppliers and partners who together form a network of relationships. Increasingly, clients are expecting the members of these networks to co-operate seamlessly to provide an integrated service or product. This requires a high level of trust between members of the network and the client. Such trust

> **'People management practices can help to overcome...barriers to integration and provide the glue to hold the KIF together.'**

does not always come naturally because of the inclination to protect commercially confidential knowledge from members of the network who may effectively be competitors.

Two kinds of people management practices are likely to be important here. The first are those concerned with developing client management skills to acquire the business and then make sure that the relationship is maintained and new business opportunities are identified. This can be difficult for certain types of knowledge worker, and it has extensive implications for both formal and informal development practices and for selection and promotion criteria. In addition, there are the skills associated with collaborating and sharing information with partners in the network. Again, sharing the explicit knowledge is not likely to be the problem as much as developing communication skills that allow the transfer of tacit knowledge.

In essence, there is an attempt here to create an information democracy (Nonaka and Takeuchi, 1995) across organisational boundaries. This might require the formation of hybrid teams made up of members from elements of the network including the client. Relations between these teams and the wider organisations will call for careful management.

Following our discussion we can now stand back and consider which of these practices really appears to make a difference to the performance of our case studies. Our analysis of this issue focused around the ability of our cases to manage three key tensions.

◻ First, it is important to satisfy the needs of individual knowledge workers for interesting work which develops their knowledge and skills

and at the same time to facilitate the transfer of knowledge between separate project teams.

◻ Second, there is the potential tension between various competing loyalties or identities – the team, organisation, profession and client. People management practices play a key role in balancing these various tensions. There may be an interplay between these tensions – for example, a strong team, professional or client identity may provide obstacles to sharing the knowledge that an organisational identity seeks to encourage. People management practices can help to overcome such barriers to integration and provide the glue to hold the KIF together.

◻ Third, these people management practices may be more effective when they have been allowed to develop inductively rather than from the top down. Successful KIFs relied on best-fit practices which evolved internally rather than being 'bought in' through a consultant. Indeed, these practices worked best when they became embedded in the organisational routines and ways of working (Ghoshal and Barlett, 1995). It was through the acceptance of these practices that a suitable balance between the team, organisational, professional and client identities was maintained.

The embedded people management practices also allowed the tension between managing knowledge workers and managing knowledge to be resolved. When practices towards recruitment, development, reward and retention were accepted internally, there were better opportunities to manage both the individual and collective dimensions of knowledge. These links between knowledge situations, people management practices and the management of these tensions

> 'Our successful firms were better able to convert human capital into intellectual capital...'

are central to the performance of the firm, and are summarised in Figure 4.

Although most of the analysis in this report has been concerned with the distinctive characteristics of KIFs, some of our broader findings have relevance to the debate on the links between people management practices and performance more generally, and in particular what has been referred to as the link between the HR advantage (Boxall and Purcell, 2003: 85) and organisational performance.

Not all our firms were equally successful, and the performance of our cases varied both in terms of performance outcomes and in their ability to share knowledge internally. Our successful firms were better able to convert human capital into intellectual capital because they had people management practices and processes that supported and enhanced this conversion process. This was not the result of chance but of clear choices about how intellectual capital and people management practices are managed. Indeed, our successful companies developed an HR advantage

which improved the conversion of human capital in such a way as to create an intellectual capital advantage.

The HR advantage is composed of both a human capital advantage (in terms of both policies and people) and a people management process advantage, which meant that formal polices were not only well designed but also were implemented by line managers in the way that was intended. The achievement of this HR advantage helps to create an intellectual capital advantage. This is made up not only of the knowledge and skills of employees but also critically of the knowledge-sharing processes within and between firms which help to maximise the benefit of the expertise for the firm.

The combination of HR and intellectual capital advantage is found in our more successful firms, and in particular it is the hard-to-imitate people management and knowledge-sharing processes that are the essence of this advantage. Both the knowledge-sharing and people management processes became embedded in the routines and

Figure 4 | The links between people management and performance

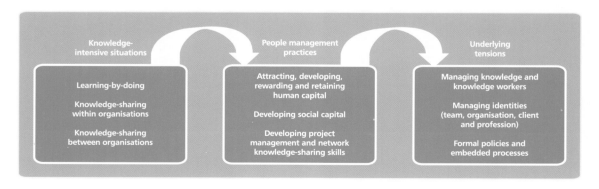

structures of the organisation in a way that is virtually impossible to copy. These mutually supportive processes became part of the core competence of the firm.

Our KIFs may well provide a guide to the situation in larger and more traditional organisations which we report on elsewhere. If we recall the knowledge-based view of strategy, we know that to some extent all organisations rely on converting their human capital into intellectual capital. There is clear evidence here of the key role which people management policies, practices and processes play in supporting the conversion of human capital into intellectual capital. The fit between the knowledge-sharing processes and people management processes is likely to be important for understanding the links between people and performance more widely.

References

ALVESSON, M. (1995)

The Management of Knowledge Intensive Companies. Berlin/New York, De Gruyter.

ALVESSON, M. (2000)

'Social identity and the problem of loyalty in knowledge intensive companies'. *Journal of Management Studies*, 37 (8), 1101–1123.

ALVESSON, M. (2001)

'Social identity and the problem of loyalty in knowledge-intensive companies'. In F. Blackler, D. Courpasson and B. Elkjaer (eds) *Knowledge Work, Organisations and Expertise: European perspectives*. London, Routledge.

ALVESSON, M. and WILLMOTT, H. (2002)

'Identity regulation as organizational control: producing the appropriate individual'. *Journal of Management Studies*, 39 (5), 619–644.

BAUMARD, P. (1999)

Tacit Knowledge in Organisations. London, Sage.

BONTIS, N. (1998)

'Intellectual capital: an exploratory study that develops measures and models'. *Management Decision*, 36 (2), 63–76.

BOXALL, P. and PURCELL, J. (2003)

Strategy and Human Resource Management. Basingstoke, Palgrave Macmillan.

BURT, R. S. (1982)

Towards a Structural Theory of Action. New York, Academic Press.

COOK, S. D. N. and SEELY BROWN, J. (1999)

'Bridging epistemologies: the generative dance between organisational knowledge and organisational knowing'. *Organization Science*, 10 (4), 381–400.

DAFT, R. L. and LEWIN, A. Y. (1993)

'Where are the theories for the new organizational form? An editorial essay'. *Organization Science, 4* (4), i –vi.

DOOREWAARD, H. and MEIHUIZEN, H. E. (2000)

'Strategic performance options in professional service organisations'. *Human Resource Management Journal*, 10 (2), 39–57.

DRUCKER, P. (1993)

Post-Capitalist Society. Oxford, Butterworth-Heinemann.

EDVINSSON, E. (2000)

'Some perspectives on intangibles and intellectual capital'. *Journal of Intellectual Capital*, 1 (1), 12–16.

FRENKEL, S. J., KORCZYNSKI, M., SHIRE, K. A. and TAM, M. (1999)

On the Front Line: Organization of work in the information economy. Ithaca, NY, Cornell UP.

GHOSHAL, S. and BARTLETT, C. A. (1995)

'Changing the role of top management: beyond structure to process'. *Harvard Business Review,* Jan-Feb, 86–96.

GRANT, R. (1991)

'The resource-based theory of competitive advantage: implications for strategy formulation'. *California Management Review*, 33 (2), 114–135.

GREINER, L. E. (1998)

'Evolution and revolution as organizations grow'. Harvard Business Review, 76 (3), 55–69.

HAMEL, G. and PRAHALAD, C. (1994)

Competing for the Future. Boston, MA, HBSP.

LATHAM, G. P. and WEXLEY, K. N. (1981)

'Increasing productivity through performance appraisal'. Reading, MA, Addison-Wesley.

LEI, D., SLOCUM, J. W. and PITTS, R. A. (1999)

'Designing organizations for competitive advantage: the power of learning and unlearning'. *Organizational Dynamics*, Winter, 24–38.

LEONARD-BARTON, D. (1995)

Wellsprings of Knowledge. Boston, MA, Harvard Business School Press.

LEV, B. (1997)

'The old rules no longer apply'. *Forbes*, 7 April.

MILLER, D. and SHAMSIE, J. (1996)

'The resource-based view of the firm in two environments: the Hollywood film studios from 1936 to 1965'. *Academy of Management Journal*, 39 (3), 519–543.

MRINALINI, N. and NATH, P. (2000)

'Organizational practices for generating human resources in non-corporate research and technology organizations'. *Journal of Intellectual Capital*, 1 (2), 177–186.

NAHAPIET, J. and GHOSHAL, S. (1998)

'Social capital, intellectual capital and the organisational advantage'. *Academy of Management Review*, 23 (2), 242–266.

NELSON, R. and WINTER, S. G. (1982)

An Evolutionary Theory of Economic Change. Cambridge, MA, Harvard University Press.

NONAKA, I. (1994)

'A dynamic theory of organizational knowledge creation'. *Organization Science*, 5 (1), 14–35.

NONAKA, I. and TAKEUCHI, H. (1995)

The Knowledge Creating Company. Oxford, Oxford University Press.

ORLIKOWSKI, W. (2002)

'Knowing in practice: enacting a collective capability in distributed organizing'. *Organization Science*, 13 (3), 249–273.

POLANYI, M. (1967)

The Tacit Dimension. London, Routledge and Kegan Paul.

QUINN, J. B. (1992)

Intelligent Enterprise. New York, The Free Press.

ROBERTSON, M. and O'MALLEY HAMMERSLEY, G. (2000)

'Knowledge management practices within a knowledge-intensive firm: the significance of the people management dimension'. *Journal of European Industrial Training*, 24 (2/3/4), 241–253.

ROBERTSON, M. and SWAN, J. (1998)

'Modes of organizing in an expert consultancy: a case study of knowledge'. *Organization*, 5 (4), 543–564.

ROBERTSON, M., SCARBROUGH, H. and SWAN, J. (1999)

'Creating knowledge within expert consulting firms: the role of organisational and institutional arrangements', Paper. Warwick Business School.

SCARBROUGH H. *et al* (1999)

Knowledge Management: A literature review. CIPD report.

SCARBROUGH, H. and SWAN, J. (2001)

'Explaining the diffusion of knowledge management: the role of fashion'. *British Journal of Management*, 12 (1–3), 3–12.

SNELL, S. A. (2002)

'Competing through Knowledge: the human capital architecture'. Paper presented at the people and perfomance conference. Bath, April 10–12.

STARBUCK, W. H. (1992)

'Learning by knowledge-intensive firms'. *Journal of Management Studies*, 3 (4), 262–275.

STEWART, T. A. (1997)

Intellectual Capital: The new wealth of organisations. New York, NY, Doubleday.

SWART, J., KINNIE, N. and PURCELL, J. (2001)

'The impact of client-relationships on organisational form and HR practices'. Paper presented at the Conference on Organisational Renewal: Challenging Human Resource Management (Theme 2, New Organisational Forms and HRM), 15 November, Nijmegen School of Management.

TSOUKAS, H. (1996)

'The firm as a distributed knowledge system: a constructionist approach'. *Strategic Management Journal,* 17, 11–25.

WENGER, E. (2000)

'Communities of practice and social learning systems'. *Organization*, 7 (2), 225–246.

YANOW, D. (1999)

'The languages of "organizational learning": a palimpsest of terms'. *Proceedings from the 3rd International Conference on Organizational Learning*, June, 1075–1086.

YOUNG, M (1995)

'Post-compulsory education and training for learning society'. *Australian and New Zealand Journal of Vocational Educational Research*.